LIVING TOGETHER PRECEDENTS

AUSTRALIA
The Law Book Company
Brisbane . Sydney . Melbourne . Perth

CANADA
Ottawa . Toronto . Calgary . Montreal . Vancouver

Agents
Steimatzky's Agency Ltd., Tel Aviv;
N.M. Tripathi (Private) Ltd., Bombay;
Eastern Law House (Private) Ltd., Calcutta;
M.P.P. House, Bangalore;
Universal Book Traders, Delhi;
Aditya Books, Delhi;
MacMillan Shuppan KK, Tokyo;
Pakistan Law House, Karachi, Lahore.

LIVING TOGETHER PRECEDENTS
Second Edition

by

JILL BOWLER BA
JACQUI JACKSON MA, LLB
EILEEN LOUGHRIDGE
Solicitors of the Supreme Court

London
Sweet & Maxwell
1994

First Edition 1989
Second Edition 1994

Published in 1994 by
Sweet and Maxwell Limited of
South Quay Plaza, 183 Marsh Wall,
London E14 9FT
Computerset by York House Typographic Ltd., London W13
Printed in Great Britain by Headway Press Ltd.

No natural forests were destroyed to
make this product: only farmed
timber was used and re-planted.

ISBN 0-421-52200-3

**A catalogue record for this book
is available from the British Library**

CONTENTS

INTRODUCTION

SECTION 1 – LIVING TOGETHER AS A COUPLE
A. AGREEMENTS

Living together agreement 1: Both parties to have share of beneficial interest in home

Recitals

The home
1. Mortgage payments
2. Capital payments in discharge of mortgage
3. Negative equity
4. Improvements
5. Non-monetary contributions
6. Major repairs
7. Replacement Home
8. Proceeds of Endowment Policies

Outgoings
9. Outgoings
10. Arrangements for payment

Contents
11. Ownership options
12. Provision for specific items
13. Items acquired on credit

Credit and loans
14. Joint bank loan, overdraft, credit cards
15. Credit cards
16. Family Loans

Other assets
17. Bank and Building Society Accounts (and other capital assets)

Pensions
18. Nominations
19. Cancellation or Alteration of Nominations

Children
20. Provision if child born
21. Maintenance Payable
22. Maintenance Received

SECTION 2 – LIVING WITH THE ELDERLY
A. AGREEMENTS

Living Together Agreement 4: All parties to have share of beneficial interest in home

Living Together Agreement 5: One party or more to retain the whole of beneficial interest in home

INTRODUCTION

INTRODUCTION

Living Together as a Couple

The living together precedents in Sections 1 to 3 are for couples who are living together but who are not married to each other. Clearly such couples can make virtually no use of the system of law available to married persons and are therefore much more vulnerable on the break up of the relationship or the death of one party. Whereas the courts have powers to adjust property rights on divorce, they can only determine who owns property and in what shares on the basis of the title deeds and documents, and, if they are unclear, actual contributions of unmarried couples and/or their intentions. It may be difficult to prove actual contributions and on separation, either or both of the parties may have honestly forgotten (or through the bitterness of the separation, may conveniently forget) their original intentions. Furthermore the law makes no provision for surviving partners on intestacy and it is even more difficult to establish contributions and intentions if one partner has died.

The aim of the precedents in this book is to provide a framework for couples to enable them to record their intentions and to provide a means of ascertaining the effects of their contributions whilst they are living happily together. This will hopefully minimise possible areas of dispute and would enable any future separation to take place with less acrimony and would as a last resort provide the court with a foundation on which to work. The authors recommend that couples be encouraged to have a living together agreement, a deed of trust in respect of the home and two wills.

Any comments on the use of the precedents in practice would be welcome.

Living with the Elderly

The precedents in Sections 2 cover the situation where people of different generations share a home, such as adult children sharing with an elderly parent or parents. This is becoming increasingly common because of the growth in an ageing and property-owning population with more families seeking to solve the problem of caring for elderly relatives by pooling resources with them.

People sharing in this way are just as vulnerable as unmarried couples in that, in the event of a dispute or the death of one party, the courts can determine ownership of assets only in accordance with the general law of property and trusts.

Various problems can arise. For example, one of the parties may die or the parties may decide to end the sharing arrangement. In the event of a death, one share of the home may be inherited by someone other than the co-owners. This may result in a dispute about how to raise the money to pay the beneficiary his or her share if the remaining co-owners wish to stay on. In the event of the parties deciding to end the sharing agreement there could be a problem sorting out who should stay and who should go and how the outgoing party's interest should be purchased. Then again, it may just be that the younger parties need to move to a different part of the country and thus bring an end to the arrangement even though they still get on well with the elderly relative. They would need to resolve how they would each realise their shares in the home if it is not to be sold.

In each of these situations possible areas of dispute would be minimised if the parties thought through the implications of the sharing arrangement and provided for as many eventualities as they can in an agreement, a deed of trust and their wills.

The living together agreement

The terms to be included in the agreement are a matter for the parties but it is important that they are fully advised, taking account of their individual circumstances, and are also made aware of areas that might not otherwise have occurred to them.

The following precedents contain clauses dealing with all the more usual and the more likely to be enforceable aspects including the property, payment of mortgage, outgoings, ownership of contents, liability for credit, ownership of bank accounts and other capital assets and provision for the termination. There are obviously many other clauses which could be included (e.g. Weitzman in *The Marriage Contract* 1981 suggests a number of other terms many of which however deal with personal rather than the financial aspects of the relationship). It is generally felt, particularly in this country, that provisions dealing with such matters could be difficult to enforce and may therefore be better avoided.

On the question of enforceability it may also be arguable whether or not the parties intend to create legal relations in such an agreement or whether it is of a purely domestic nature. Precise terms and detailed particularisation of the matters relating to cohabitation in addition to the statement of intention to create legal relations should ensure enforceability. It is, however, important to exclude from the agreement any language which would support the conclusion that the purpose of the agreement is to provide for a sexual relationship and which would cause the agreement to run the risk of unenforceability on the grounds of being contrary to public policy. Enforceability is unlikely to be a problem in sharing arrangements with the elderly.

Also to avoid any uncertainty about the presence of consideration in any particular living together agreement it is suggested that the agreement should always be by deed.

Living together agreement precedents 1 and 4 are for those wishing to share the beneficial interest in their home either in a presently owned property or an intended purchase where the legal title is in joint names or sole name and where the beneficial interest can be held in any one of nine different ways. Precedent 2 is a living together agreement where the parties are renting. Finally, living together agreement precedents 3 and 5 are for use where the legal and beneficial ownership is vested in one person or more and it is agreed that the other party or parties will not acquire any interest no matter what contribution is made.

The deed of trust

The trust deed sets out the legal ownership and respective beneficial interests in the home. It may not be necessary if the legal title and beneficial ownership have clearly been dealt with in the conveyance or transfer to the parties but obviously will be essential if the legal title is not to be in the names of all the parties. It will be desirable if the parties wish the beneficial shares to be other than equal or simple percentages (for example to take account of previous or future contributions and/or discounts) since this will enable complex provisions to be kept off the title.

In all cases the title deeds should be examined to check whether the beneficial interest is clearly defined (there have been reported cases where a conveyance to joint owners has not contained any express declaration of trust as to the respective beneficial interests).

Readers should be particularly careful to advise clients fully about the relative merits of joint tenancies and tenancies in common taking account of "as much of their background and surrounding circumstances as can reasonably be ascertained" since failure to do so may amount to negligence – see in particular *Taylor v. Harman and Warners* (Law Society Gazette number 25 1988). Sections 2 and 4 set out precedents of trust deeds for property in joint names or in sole name.

Wills

It is essential that couples living together both make wills particularly because of the lack of protection under the Intestacy Rules. If one or other already has a will then this should be checked to ensure it is appropriate for the couple's present circumstances, especially where one or both of the partners has pre-existing obligations such as children from a previous marriage or relationship.

Couples should be advised about the consequences of failing to appoint executors, the possibilities of appointing guardians, the benefits of outright gifts even if provision is to be made for children and of giving a surviving partner time to find other accommodation. In section 3 there are precedents of some useful clauses to be incorporated into readers' existing will precedents.

As most company pension and private pension schemes do not automatically form part of a testator's estate, cohabitees should be advised to find out from the administrator of any such scheme, of which they are a member, to whom any payment would be made on death and, if necessary, to revise nomination instructions.

In any sharing arrangements with the elderly the parties will almost inevitably want to hold as tenants-in-common and therefore will need to make wills. This is particularly important where, for example, one party, the parent, wishes to leave his or her estate to be divided among all the children and not just the child he or she is sharing with. Careful consideration needs to be given when drafting the wills to protect all parties and potential beneficiaries.

Miscellaneous

We have found in practice that several other documents may be called for when dealing with clients who are sharing a home. We thought it would be helpful to add to this edition the prescribed form for a Parental Responsibility Agreement, a simple form of appointment of a guardian and a Memorandum of Gift, where a third party is providing funds.

Due to the possibility of future mental or physical incapacity, the elderly client should be advised to consider completing an Enduring Power of Attorney and, possibly, the appointment of a personal care decision maker.

The Enduring Powers of Attorney Act 1985 enables a person to appoint one or more attorneys to deal with his or her financial affairs and property. The Power must be in the prescribed form as set out in Section 4. It can be used as a general power unless and until the Attorney believes that the Donor is or is becoming mentally incapacitated at which point the Power must be registered with the Court of Protection. Because of the scope for misuse, extreme care should be taken in choosing an Attorney and in deciding the limits of that Attorney's authority.

The two precedents for the appointment of a personal care decision maker are intended to cover non-financial decisions in the event of future incapacity, such as where the Appointor is to reside. At present the appointment of a person to make such decisions may not be enforceable but the Law Commission Consultation Paper No. 128, *Mentally Incapacitated Adults and Decision Making: An Overview* favours legislation to enable such appointments to be made.

The precedents are based on the law as at March 1, 1994.

SECTION 1

LIVING TOGETHER AS A COUPLE

A.
AGREEMENTS

LIVING TOGETHER AGREEMENT 1: BOTH PARTIES TO HAVE SHARE OF BENEFICIAL INTEREST IN HOME

THIS DEED OF AGREEMENT is made the .... day of 19

BETWEEN:

1. *[name* ....*]* of *[address* ....*]* ("*[A]*") and

2. *[name* ....*]* of *[address* ....*]* ("*[B]*")

WHEREAS:

(1) The parties [live together] [intend to live together]

(2) The parties wish to enter into an agreement regulating their rights and obligations towards each other and towards any children of the relationship and of any previous relationship

(3) The parties intend that this Agreement shall be legally binding on them

(4) The parties declare that they have each had the benefit of independent legal advice prior to the execution of this agreement and are signing it voluntarily and in full understanding of their respective rights and liabilities hereunder.

OR

(4) The parties declare that they have been advised to seek independent legal advice but have declined to do so.

(5) The parties presently have no children

OR

(5) The parties presently have *[number]* child[ren] namely:

(a) *[name(s)..................]* being the child[ren] of the relationship [of whom *[number]* are] presently under the age of majority

(b) *A* has *[number]* child[ren] namely *[name(s)..................]* being the child[ren] of a previous relationship [of whom *[number]* are] presently under the age of majority

(c) *B* has *[number]* child[ren] namely *[name(s)* ....*]* being the child[ren] of a previous relationship [of whom *[number]* are] presently under the age of majority

The Home – Legal Title

Legal Title – Existing Property

(6) The parties are presently resident at the address given above ("the Home") which is a property purchased [in their joint names] [in the sole name of..]

OR

Legal Title – Property to be Purchased

(6) The parties are presently resident at the address[es] given above but intend to purchase a property ("the Home") [in their joint names] [in the sole name of..] the address of which is *[address of property to be purchased]*

The Home – Beneficial Interest

NOTE: It is suggested that in most cases couples entering into a living together agreement will also execute a deed of trust setting out their respective beneficial interests in the home. This will of course be essential if the agreed beneficial interests are to be varied from the provisions in the conveyance/transfer of the property on purchase.

If a deed of trust is not to be executed then recital 7 will need to refer instead to the beneficial interests as contained in the conveyance/transfer of the property to the parties or to one of them.

(7) The parties intend to enter into a Deed of Trust which will provide as follows:

Option A: Joint Tenants

They [are] [shall be] entitled to the beneficial interest in the Home as joint tenants in equity.

OR

Option B: Equal Shares

Regardless of their respective contributions to the purchase price of the Home they [are] [shall be] entitled to the beneficial interest in the Home in equal shares

OR

Option C: % Shares

Regardless of their respective contributions to the purchase price of the Home they [are] [shall be] entitled to the beneficial interest in the Home as to *[number]* % to *A* and as to *[number]* % to *B*

OR

Option D: Shares in Proportion to Contributions to Purchase Price/Mortgage

They are and shall be entitled to the beneficial interest in the Home in the proportions in which they contribute to the purchase of the Home whether by way of payment of mortgage instalments and mortgage-linked endowment policy premiums as set out in Clause 1 and/or by way of future lump sum payment as set out in Clauses 2 and 4

OR

Option E: Provision for previous contributions by one or both parties to be taken into account. Remainder in accordance with agreement or in stated shares

(a) From the date hereof they shall be entitled to the beneficial interest in the Home calculated on the basis that

A is entitled to a sum equal to *[number]* % of the sale price before deductions or ....pounds (£......................................) whichever is the greater as a result of having paid £.............

AND/OR

B is entitled to a sum equal to *[number]* % of the sale price before deductions or ....pounds (£..) whichever is the greater as a result of having paid £..

AND/OR

[name] is entitled to a sum equal to *[number]* % of the sale price before deductions or ....pounds (£..) whichever is the greater as a result of having obtained a discount in the purchase price due to [his] [her] prior occupation of the Home as a tenant

AND/OR

[name] is entitled to a sum equal to *[number]* % of the sale price before deductions or ....pounds (£..) whichever is the greater as a result of having obtained a reduction in the purchase price as a benefit from [his] [her] family

(b) and the remainder shall be held in the proportions in which they contribute to the purchase of the Home whether by way of payment of mortgage instalments and mortgage-linked endowment policy premiums as set out in Clause 1 and/or by way of future lump sum payment as set out in Clauses 2 and 4

OR

(b) and the remainder shall be held as to *[number]* % for *A* and as to *[number]* % for *B*

NOTE: Option E(a) records contributions made by either or both parties prior to the date of the agreement either by lump sum payment and/or discount under a "right to buy" tenancy or because of a reduction in the purchase price of a property purchased from a member of the family (e.g. where a parent has inherited a house he/she may agree a sale below market value).

Option E(b) allows alternative ways of dealing with the remainder of the equity. Extreme care needs to be taken when calculating the respective shares of the parties so as to take account of a lump sum payment and/or discount by one party as at the date of the agreement. If either party wishes to preserve a percentage it must be clearly shown whether such percentage is to be calculated by reference to the eventual sale price or to net proceeds after deductions including mortgage since otherwise there may be, at best, ambiguity and at worst an unintended result.

OR

Option F: Sole Name. That Party to have Benefit of Value to date. Remainder in accordance with this Agreement

[Name of non-owning party] is not entitled to any beneficial interest as at the date of this Agreement. The agreed value of the Home less the amount outstanding on the mortgage as at the date hereof is................pounds (£...) and *[name of owning party]* shall be entitled to this sum out of any net proceeds of sale before division and in addition to any further share to which s/he may become entitled under the terms of this Agreement. From the date of this Agreement *[name of non-owning party]* shall acquire a beneficial interest and hereafter the parties shall be entitled to the beneficial interest in the proportions in which they contribute to the purchase of the Home whether by way of payment of mortgage

instalments and mortgage-linked endowment policy premiums as set out in Clause 1 and/or by way of future lump sum payment as set out in Clauses 2 and 4

OR

Option G: Sole Name. That party to have Benefit of Value at date of Commencement of Cohabitation. Remainder in accordance with this Agreement

At the commencement of cohabitation on or about *[date] [name of non-owning party]* had no beneficial interest in the Home. The agreed value of the Home less the amount outstanding on the mortgage as at the said date was................pounds (£ ....) and *[name of owning party]* shall be entitled to this sum out of any net proceeds of sale before division and in addition to any further share to which s/he may become entitled under the terms of this Agreement. From the said date *[name of non-owning party]* acquired a beneficial interest and the parties are and shall be entitled to the beneficial interest in the proportions in which they contribute to the purchase of the Home whether by way of payment of mortgage instalments and mortgage-linked endowment policy premiums as set out in Clause 1 and/or by way of future lump sum payment as set out in Clauses 2 and 4

OR

Option H: Sole name. That party to have Benefit of Value to date. Remainder in stated shares

[Name of non-owning party] is not entitled to any beneficial interest as at the date of this Agreement].

The agreed value of the Home less the amount outstanding on the mortgage as at the date hereof is...............pounds (£..) and *[name of owning party]* shall be entitled to this sum out of any net proceeds of sale before division and in addition to [his] [her] percentage share in any increase in the value of the Home over and above the said sum. The parties declare that from the date of this Agreement they are entitled to the beneficial interest in any increase in the value of the Home over and above the said sum [in equal shares] [as to *number* % to *A* and as to *number* % to *B*]

OR

Option I: Sole Name. That party to have Benefit of Value at Date of Commencement of Cohabitation. Remainder in stated shares

At the commencement of cohabitation on or about *[date] [name of non-owning party]* had no beneficial interest in the Home. The agreed value of the Home less the amount outstanding on the mortgage at the commencement of cohabitation on or about *[date]* was............pounds (£................) and *[name of owning party]* shall be entitled to this sum out of any net proceeds of sale before division and in addition to [his] [her] percentage share in any increase in the value of the Home over and above the said sum. The parties declare that they are entitled to the beneficial interest in any increase in the value of the Home over and above the said sum [in equal shares] [as to *number* % to *A* and as to *number* % to *B*]

NOTE: Options F to I deal with the situation where the property was in the sole name of one party prior to commencement of cohabitation and the value of the equity at that time is to be preserved for that party. The difference between F and G is to cater for the fact that the parties may be making this agreement when they commence cohabitation or some time later. The difference between F/G and H/I is to allow parties alternative ways of dealing with the equity from commencement of cohabitation onwards.

The Home

1. Mortgage payment options

Half Each

(1) Each party shall pay half the mortgage repayments [and half the mortgage-linked endowment policy premiums]

OR

% Payment

(1) The mortgage repayments [and mortgage-linked endowment policy premiums] shall be paid as to *[number]* % by *A* and as to *[number]* % by *B*

OR

Payment by one

(1) The mortgage repayments [and mortgage-linked endowment policy premiums] shall be paid by *[name]* alone

> *NOTE: If the parties are to own the beneficial interest in the home in accordance with options D, E, F or G of clause 7 of the recitals, the percentage payments stated here will determine the proportions in which they are to be entitled to the beneficial interest (subject to the provisions dealing with future lump sum payments and improvements). Failure to pay will not affect this.*

OR

Payment by agreement

(1) The mortgage repayments [and mortgage-linked endowment policy premiums] shall be paid as agreed from time to time between the parties SAVE that it is further agreed that the proportions in which they hold the beneficial interest in the Home shall be calculated by reference to the actual payments made by each

> *NOTE: This clause can be used if the parties wish the proportions in which they hold the beneficial interest to be calculated by reference to the actual payments made by each BUT it should be made clear that it would be necessary to keep careful and complete proof of such payments. If this option is chosen the sub clause (2) "Failure to pay" should be omitted.*

Failure to pay

(2) If one party shall fail to pay [his] [her] share of the mortgage and mortgage-linked endowment policy premiums for whatever reason and the other party shall pay that share in addition to [his] [her] own share then notwithstanding such failure to pay it is agreed that the respective shares of the parties in the beneficial interest in the Home shall remain unaltered

> *NOTE: Without this clause, if one party failed to pay his or her agreed share for whatever reason, the beneficial interest would be subject to change and could only be calculated in any subsequent dispute by extensive investigation of actual payments made by each party. The clause, therefore, provides certainty, but it should be made clear to the parties the position if one does not pay the agreed share.*

2. Capital payments in discharge of Mortgage

Where either party makes a capital payment in discharge or part discharge of any mortgage secured on the Home that party's percentage share in the beneficial interest in the Home shall be adjusted to reflect such capital payment. The adjusted percentage shall be calculated by reference to the value of the Home at the time of such payment such value to be agreed between the parties and, if not so agreed, determined by a Valuer appointed jointly by the parties or in default by a Valuer to be appointed by the President for the time being of the Royal Institution of Chartered

Surveyors. The particulars of such adjustments shall be recorded in accordance with the variation Clause

> *NOTE: It is important that any variation is recorded at the time such payment is made and the parties should be advised accordingly.*

3. Negative Equity

(1) Where on any sale of the Home the liability remaining outstanding on the mortgage exceeds the proceeds of sale, then in the absence of any written agreement to the contrary such liability shall be borne by the parties in the proportions in which they hold the beneficial interest in the Home.

(2) Where on any transfer of the Home from one party to the other the liability remaining outstanding on the mortgage exceeds the value of the Home, then in the absence of any written agreement to the contrary such deficit shall be borne by the parties in the proportions in which they hold the beneficial interest in the Home. The value of the Home shall be agreed between the parties, and if not so agreed determined by a Valuer appointed jointly by the parties or in default by a Valuer to be appointed by the President for the time being of the Royal Institution of Chartered Surveyors.

4. Improvements

Improvements which add to the value of the Home shall not be undertaken except by prior agreement between the parties. Where either party makes a contribution by payment for or part payment for such previously agreed improvements which increase the value of the Home that party's percentage share in the beneficial interest in the Home shall be adjusted to reflect such contribution. The increase in value and the adjusted percentage shall be calculated by reference to the value of the Home at the time of such payment such value to be agreed between the parties and, if not so agreed, determined by a Valuer to be appointed jointly by the parties and in default by a Valuer to be appointed by the President for the time being of the Royal Institution of Chartered Surveyors. The particulars of such adjustments shall be recorded in accordance with the variation Clause.

> *NOTE: The parties should be advised of the need to have the property valued at the time the improvement is made.*

5. Non-monetary contributions

Where a party makes a non-monetary contribution which increases the value of the Home such a contribution shall not affect that party's beneficial interest in the Home unless the parties agree in advance that that party's share shall thereby be increased. The particulars of such agreed increase shall be recorded in accordance with the variation Clause.

> *NOTE: Because of the disparity in judgments in reported cases as to what amounts to a non-monetary contribution sufficient to affect the beneficial interest in the home, it is suggested that this clause be included by which the parties agree that such a non-monetary contribution shall not affect the beneficial interest of the party making the contribution unless they agree in advance that it should.*

6. Major Repairs

(1) Any repair to the Home the cost of which will, or is likely to, exceed £1,000.00 shall not be undertaken except by prior agreement between the parties and if the cost does exceed that sum it shall be funded as agreed between the parties at the time the repair is undertaken and in default of such agreement it shall be funded [equally] [as to *number* % by *A* and as to *number* % by *B*] [by *name* alone]

(2) Contributions to the funding of any repairs to the Home shall not entitle the payer[s] to any share or increased share in the beneficial interest in the Home

(3) Where the parties agree at the time that a repair to the Home is undertaken that such repair is to be treated as an improvement then the provisions of Clause 4 shall apply in place of sub clause (1) and (2) above

NOTE: The figure of £1,000 is included as an example only and can be any figure chosen by the parties.

7. Replacement Home

(1) Where the parties acquire a property to replace the Home they shall enter into a declaration of trust at the time of purchase setting out their respective beneficial interests in the replacement home (the declaration to be contained in the Conveyance or Transfer or Lease or Assignment of the replacement home to the parties or either of them and/or to be contained in a separate Deed entered into by the parties)

(2) In default of any such Deed of Trust and in the absence of any express contrary provision in the said Conveyance Transfer Lease or Assignment the beneficial interest in the replacement home shall be held in the same proportions as the beneficial interest in the Home at the date of sale

NOTE: There have been cases where there was no express declaration of trust in the conveyance or transfer of the property as to the beneficial interest and this clause has been included to ensure that even in such a situation the beneficial interest is still clear.

8. Proceeds of Endowment Policies

The parties agree that the proceeds of any mortgage-linked endowment policy on their joint lives shall be applied first in or towards redemption of any mortgage or mortgages secured on the Home and any surplus following such redemption shall belong to the parties in the same proportions as the beneficial interest in the Home.

Outgoings

9. Outgoings

Common household expenditure including Council Tax or other local tax, water rates, gas, electricity, telephone, television licence and/or rental agreement, buildings household and contents insurance, food, decorating and repairs costing less than £1,000.00 shall be paid [equally] [as to *number* % by *A* and as to *number* % by *B*] [by *name* alone]. [This provision shall also apply to payment of ground rent service charge(s) insurance premiums and any other sums due under the terms of any Lease by virtue of which the parties occupy the Home)

NOTE: This list is not exhaustive and can be amended to suit clients' individual requirements.

10. Arrangements for payment

The parties declare that notwithstanding the practical arrangements made by them as between themselves for actual payment in respect of the mortgage endowment policy premiums and common household expenditure their respective interests in the Home are as set out in Clause (7) of the recitals hereof

NOTE: The parties may, for practical reasons, decide to have separate accounts so that, for example, one makes all the mortgage payments and the other the common household expenses. This clause is to make it clear that such practical arrangements will not affect the beneficial interest.

Contents

11. Ownership of contents options

Sole

(1) All items of personal use or adornment shall belong to the party who last acquired them whether by inheritance gift or purchase and where the acquisition of any such item was financed

by any credit facility in the name of the other party or in the joint names of the parties it shall nonetheless be considered to be solely the property of the party acquiring it and the subsequent provisions of this Agreement shall have no effect as regards items of personal use or adornment

Joint

(2) Subject to Clauses 12, 13 and 14 below and except as may be specified in the Schedule hereto all furniture household garden or garage articles or effects and electrical equipment ("the Contents") shall be considered to be owned jointly regardless of when or by whom they were acquired

OR

Belong to party who acquired them

(2) Subject to Clauses 12, 13 and 14 below and except as may be specified in the Schedule hereto all furniture household garden or garage articles or effects and electrical equipment ("the Contents") shall belong to the party who last acquired them whether by inheritance gift or purchase

OR

All items over £............belong to person who acquired them

(2) Subject to Clauses 12, 13 and 14 below and except as may be specified in the Schedule hereto all furniture household garden or garage articles or effects and electrical equipment ("the Contents") shall if worth over.................pounds (£................) at the date of termination of this Agreement belong to the party who last acquired them whether by inheritance gift or purchase and all other items shall be considered to be owned jointly

Motor Vehicle – sole

(3) Any motor vehicle shall belong to the party who acquired it

OR

Motor Vehicle – joint

(3) Any motor vehicle shall be considered to be owned jointly regardless of when or by whom it was acquired except that any motor vehicle which at the date of termination of this Agreement shall be subject to any form of finance or credit agreement hire purchase or loan in the name of one party shall (be) (or be deemed to be) the property of the party liable under the Agreement

12. Provisions for specific items to be dealt with separately

If there should be particular items within Clause 11 above which the parties wish to own jointly such items shall be listed on a schedule and signed by both parties and thereafter they shall be considered to be owned jointly

OR

If there should be particular items within Clause 11 above which the parties agree shall be owned by one of them alone such items shall be listed on a Schedule and signed by both parties and thereafter they shall be considered to be owned by that party

NOTE: If the second or third option of 11(2) is chosen then alternative one above is needed. If the first option of 11(2) is chosen then alternative two is required.

13. Items acquired on credit

By one party

(1) All items acquired by one party before or during the period of cohabitation and which are subject to any form of finance or credit agreement hire purchase or loan shall [be] [be deemed to be] the property of the party liable under the finance or credit agreement hire purchase or loan and that party shall be responsible for making all the repayments

NOTE: The reason for this clause is that often situations arise where one party has acquired an item on credit but then leaves that item with the other party on separation and neither party wants to continue to make the credit payments. Credit agreements are rarely, if ever, assignable. By having this clause in the agreement both parties are thereby aware that any items acquired on credit belong to that party and that party remains responsible for the payments.

Jointly

(2) All items acquired jointly during the period of cohabitation and which are subject to any form of finance or credit agreement hire purchase or loan shall [be] [be deemed to be] the joint property of the parties and the parties shall be jointly responsible for making all the repayments

NOTE: Items acquired before cohabitation have been included because often couples buy items on credit with a view to living together or bring such items to the relationship. This does not affect the parties' joint and several liability to the lender.

Credit and loans

14. Joint Bank loan, overdraft, credit card

All items costing over................pounds (£ ....) acquired either before or during the period of cohabitation the purchase of which is financed by a joint bank loan or overdraft facility joint credit card or credit card in the sole name of one party and of which the other party is authorised user or any other joint credit facility shall be considered to be owned jointly

NOTE: This was included to cover any other items which are not the specific subject of a finance agreement but which are in effect acquired on joint credit. It is essential to specify a minimum figure to avoid arguments arising over small credit card purchases.

15. Credit Cards

Sole name

(1) All payments made pursuant to any credit card agreement or other finance or revolving credit agreement or loan facility (other than mortgage repayments and as provided in Clause 13 above) which is in the sole name of one party shall be made [by that party] [equally] [as to *number* % by *A* and as to *number* % by *B*]

Joint/authorised user

(2) All payments made pursuant to any credit card agreement or other finance or revolving credit agreement or loan facility (other than mortgage repayments and as provided in Clause 13 above) which is in the joint names of the parties or a credit card agreement in the sole name of one party of which the other party is an authorised user shall be made [equally] [as to *number* % by *A* and as to *number* % by *B*] [by *name* alone]

NOTE: This provides for the parties to agree as between themselves as to how they are going to be responsible for the repayments on credit cards. It will not of course affect the liability of the card holder vis-a-vis the lender.

16. Family Loans

Joint Liability

(1) Any existing or future loans received from the family of either party shall be considered to be the joint liability of the parties and repayments shall be made [equally] [as to *number* % by *A* and as to *number* % by *B*] [by *name* alone]

OR

Sole Liability

(1) Any existing or future loans received from the family of either party shall be considered to be the sole liability of *[name]* and repayments shall be made [equally] [as to *number* % by *A* and as to *number* % by *B*] [by *name* alone]

Existing Loans

(2) The parties declare that [they have] *[name]* [has] received a loan of £.............from *[name of lender]* repayable [on demand][by *[number]* instalments payable [monthly in advance][monthly in arrear]][interest-free][subject to interest of........% per cent per annum]

NOTE: This is designed to focus the minds of the parties on loans from the family of one or both of them. This will ensure that both parties and hopefully their families are clear who is responsible for repayments. Strictly it does not affect the liability of the couple vis-a-vis the family but might have some evidential value. This clause has nothing to do with recital (7) E (a) fourth option.

Other assets

17. Bank and Building Society Accounts (and other capital assets)

Joint

(1) Any joint Bank or Building Society account the parties may have or may establish whether for the purpose of paying the expenses hereinbefore referred to or for any other purpose and any other jointly owned investment or capital asset (excluding the Home and Contents as hereinbefore defined and motor vehicles) shall belong to the parties [in equal shares] [as to *number* % to *A* and as to *number* % to *B*] irrespective of the proportions in which they contributed to the account or investment or acquisition of the asset.

AND

Sole

(2) Any Bank or Building Society account and any other investment or capital asset (excluding the Home and Contents as hereinbefore defined and motor vehicles) in the sole name of either party shall remain the property of that party

NOTE: Many people believe that joint bank accounts mean that the account holders are equally entitled to the money in the account. This is not true and in the absence of express agreement it could be difficult to justify who should have what. This can be particularly difficult if one party dies and banks have been known to freeze accounts leaving the survivor without access to any money. This clause also covers any other investment or capital asset.

Pensions

18. Nominations

The parties will each nominate the other to receive [the whole] [*number* %] of the death in service benefits pension and/or other payments due under any pension scheme or schemes of which he or she may from time to time be a member.

19. Cancellation or Alteration of Nominations

Except on termination or variation of this Agreement any nomination made under the provisions of Clause 18 hereof shall not be cancelled or altered save with the prior written consent of the other party.

Children

20. Provisions for payment if child born

Fixed period

In the event of the parties suffering a reduction in income as a result of *[name]* having a child by *[name]* he shall pay all the expenses hereinbefore referred to for *[number]* months and such payments shall not affect their respective beneficial interests in the Home

OR

Agreed period

In the event of the parties suffering a reduction in income as a result of *[name]* having a child by *[name]* he shall pay all the expenses hereinbefore referred to for such period as shall be agreed between them and such payments shall not affect their respective beneficial interests in the Home

21. Maintenance Payable

Sole

Maintenance payable to or for a child or children of a previous relationship of one party by that party shall be paid by that party

OR

Joint

Maintenance payable to or for a child or children of a previous relationship of one party by that party shall be treated as part of common household expenditure referred to in Clause 9 above and shall be paid accordingly

22. Maintenance Received

Maintenance received for a child or children of a previous relationship of one party shall be used for the benefit of that child or children.

Disputes

23. Dispute resolution

If there should be any dispute between the parties concerning this agreement (other than disputes about valuation when the provisions for resolution of such disputes contained elsewhere in this agreement shall apply) either during the subsistence of this agreement or upon termination hereof which the parties are not able to resolve themselves, they agree to refer such dispute to [mutually convenient mediators of the Family Mediators Association] [a mutually convenient office of National Family Mediation] whilst reserving the right to refer the matter to the Court for adjudication if resolution of the dispute should not prove possible.

Termination/variation

24. Termination

This Agreement shall terminate on the happening of any of the following:

(a) The death of either party

(b) The marriage of the parties to each other

(c) Notice in writing given by one party to the other whereupon the transitional provisions below shall apply

(d) The parties agreeing mutually to cease to leave together whereupon the transitional provisions below shall apply

(e) The abandonment of the Home by one party and such abandonment being deemed by the other party to terminate the relationship whereupon the transitional provisions below shall apply

Transitional provisions

In the event of this Agreement being terminated, except by death or marriage of the parties to each other, the following transitional provisions shall apply:

(1) If either party wishes to remain in the Home he or she shall be given a period of four months from the termination of the Agreement within which to complete the purchase of the other party's interest in the Home

NOTE: A period of four months was inserted as being the minimum reasonable period by which one party could make all the necessary financing arrangements to complete the purchases of the other party's interest whilst ensuring that the matter does not drag on for too long. However an alternative period can be inserted. The clause is suitable where it is clear that only one party wishes to stay.

(2) If both parties wish to remain in the Home preference shall be given to that party with whom any children of the relationship or of any previous relationship will reside. If that party cannot raise the necessary funds then the other party shall be given the opportunity of doing so.

NOTE: If there are children then it is felt that preference should be given to the party with whom they will reside. If the parties are prepared to agree that the party with whom the children will reside should be allowed to remain in the home until the children reach 17 or cease full time education then a clause can be included but it is felt that this could cause disputes over who the children should live with.

If such a clause is included the parties may wish to state in a recital the purpose of the trust in order to provide certainty and to avoid any contested applications for an order for sale by one of the parties. The purpose may be, for example, that it is intended to provide a home during the minority of the children of one or both the parties or, alternatively, that the home was purchased as an investment. This requires very serious consideration and, preferably, independent legal advice as, in the event of separation or death, it may prevent one party, or his or her Personal Representatives, realising their interest in the home for an extremely long time.

First able to complete

(3) If both parties wish to remain in the Home, and there are no children, then the first of them to provide written evidence that a mortgage offer and/or cleared funds are available to that party shall be entitled to purchase the other party's interest, such purchase to be completed within one month thereafter

OR

Preference to legal owner

(3) If both parties wish to remain in the Home, and there are no children, then preference shall be given to the party in whose name the legal title is vested. If that party cannot raise the necessary funds then the other party shall be given the opportunity of doing so.

NOTE: This alternative will be the more appropriate where the legal title is in one name only.

(4) The purchasing party shall take all necessary steps to obtain the release of the selling party from all liability under the existing Mortgage[s] (if any)

(5) The value of the Home shall be the fair market value with vacant possession (and each party's share shall be valued proportionately without reference to the joint ownership) placed upon it by a Valuer agreed between the parties and in default appointed by the President for the time being of the Royal Institution of Chartered Surveyors

(6) If neither party wishes to remain in the Home, or if any party wishing to remain in the Home is unable to complete the purchase within the specified period, the Home shall be sold for the best price reasonably obtainable as agreed between the parties or certified by the selling agent and in default by a Valuer appointed by the President for the time being of the Royal Institution of Chartered Surveyors and the net proceeds shall be divided between the parties in accordance with their beneficial interests as hereinbefore provided

Mortgage payments as agreement

(7) Until sale of the Home or the transfer of the Home into the sole name of one party, the Mortgage shall continue to be paid as set out in Clause 1 above

OR

Mortgage payments by occupier

(7) Until sale of the Home or the transfer of the Home into the sole name of one party, the Mortgage shall be paid by the party remaining in occupation until sale or transfer credit being given to that party for payment over and above [his][her] own share.

(8) Common household expenditure including any of the items as identified in Clause 9 hereof accruing from the date of separation until sale of the Home or the transfer of the Home into the sole name of one party shall be paid by the party remaining in occupation

NOTE: Council Tax and water rates often cause a problem. The parties should decide in advance how they want them treated.

(9) Any Contents and motor vehicles and any Bank or Building Society accounts or other capital assets owned jointly shall be divided equally be agreement between the parties and in default of agreement shall be sold and realised and/or the proceeds divided equally

NOTE: Couples should be advised that they will both remain liable for repayments in respect of contents subject to finance and credit agreement, hire purchase or loan whoever retains the item.

(10) The parties shall take immediate steps to terminate the use of any credit card agreement or other finance or revolving credit agreement in the joint names of the parties or in the sole name of one party where the other party is an authorised user and whether or not such agreement has been terminated the parties shall be liable for the balance due under such agreement together with accrued interest in the proportions in which they made payments under Clause 15. If either party should obtain further credit after the date of separation that party shall remain solely liable for repayment together with accrued interest

Repayments as agreement

(11) Any loans from the family of either party outstanding at the date of termination shall continue to be repaid in accordance with Clause 16 above

OR

Repayments within family

(11) Any loans from the family of either party outstanding at the date of termination shall be repaid by the party from whose family the loan was received.

(12) Any nomination or nominations in respect of any pension scheme or schemes made by either party under Clause 18 hereof shall be deemed to have been cancelled as from the date of termination

NOTE: Couples should be advised to take all necessary steps to notify pension fund administrators that such nominations are to be cancelled.

(13) *A* and/or *B* shall pay maintenance to any child or children of the relationship at a rate to be agreed between the parties until the said child or children attain[s] the age of 17 years or if later cease[s] full time education and/or training

NOTE: Any such agreement would be subject to a Child Support Agency assessment.

26. Variation

Any variation of this Agreement and any adjustment in the respective shares of the parties in the beneficial interest in the Home pursuant to Clauses 2, 4 and 5 shall only be effective if recorded in a supplemental written agreement executed by both parties.

IN WITNESS whereof the parties hereto have hereunto set their hands the day and year first before written

SCHEDULE

Contents

It is hereby agreed that notwithstanding the Contents Clause herein the following items shall be considered to be owned by *[name]*

[LIST]

SIGNED AS A DEED
by the said

in the presence of

SIGNED AS A DEED
by the said

in the presence of

LIVING TOGETHER AGREEMENT 2: HOME RENTED

THIS DEED OF AGREEMENT is made the .... day of .... 19.....

BETWEEN:

1. *[name* ....*]* of *[address*..*]* ("*[A]*") and

2. *[name* ....*]* of *[address*..*]* ("*[B]*")

WHEREAS

(1) The parties [live together] [intend to live together]

(2) The parties wish to enter into an agreement regulating their rights and obligations towards each other and towards any children of the relationship and of any previous relationship

(3) The parties intend that this Agreement shall be legally binding on them

(4) The parties declare that they have each had the benefit of independent legal advice prior to the execution of this agreement and are signing it voluntarily and in full understanding of their respective rights and liabilities hereunder.

OR

(4) The parties declare that they have been advised to seek independent legal advice but have declined to do so.

(5) The parties presently have no children.

OR

(5) The parties presently have *[number]* child[ren] namely:

(a) *[name(s)]* being the child[ren] of the relationship [of whom *[number]* are] presently under the age of majority

(b) *A* has *[number]* child[ren] namely *[name(s)]* being the child[ren] of a previous relationship [of whom *[number]* are] presently under the age of majority

(c) *B* has *[number]* child[ren] namely *[name(s)]* being the child[ren] of a previous relationship [of whom *[number]* are] presently under the age of majority

The Home

Present Tenancy

(6) The parties are presently resident at the address given above ("the Home") which is a property rented in [their joint names] [the sole name of *name*]

OR

Future Tenancy

(6) The parties are presently resident at the address[es] given above but intend to rent a property ("the Home") [in their joint names] [in the sole name of *name*] the address of which is *[address]*

IT IS HEREBY AGREED as follows:

The home

1. Rent

Each party shall pay half the rent

OR

The rent shall be paid as to *number* % by *A* and as to *number* % by *B*

OR

The rent shall be paid by *[name]* alone

Outgoings

2. Outgoings

Common household expenditure including Council Tax or other local tax, water rates, gas, electricity, telephone, television licence and/or rental agreement, buildings household and contents insurance, food, decorating and repairs shall be paid [equally] [as to *number* % by A and as to *number* % by *B*] [by *name* alone]

NOTE: See note agreement 1 clause 9

Contents

3. Ownership of contents Options

Sole

(1) All items of personal use or adornment shall belong to the party who last acquired them whether by inheritance gift or purchase and where the acquisition of any such items was financed by any Credit facility in the name of the other party or in the joint names of the parties it shall nonetheless be considered to be solely the property of the party acquiring it and the subsequent provisions of this Agreement shall have no effect as regards items of personal use or adornment

Joint

(2) Subject to Clauses 4, 5 and 6 below and except as may be specified in the Schedule hereto all furniture household garden or garage articles or effects and electrical equipment ("the Contents") shall be considered to be owned jointly regardless of when or by whom they were acquired

OR

Belong to the party who acquired them

(2) Subject to Clauses 4, 5 and 6 below and except as may be specified in the Schedule hereto all furniture household garden or garage articles or effects and electrical equipment ("the

Contents") shall belong to the party who last acquired them whether by inheritance gift or purchase

OR

All items over £............ belong to person who acquired them

(2) Subject to Clauses 4, 5 and 6 below and except as may be specified in the Schedule hereto all furniture household garden or garage articles or effects and electrical equipment ("the Contents") shall if worth over................pounds (£ ....) at the date of termination of this Agreement belong to the party who last acquired them whether by inheritance gift or purchase and all other items shall be considered to be owned jointly.

Motor Vehicle – sole

(3) Any motor vehicle shall belong to the party who acquired it

OR

Motor Vehicle – joint

(3) Any motor vehicle shall be considered to be owned jointly regardless of when or by whom it was acquired except that any motor vehicle which at the date of termination of this Agreement shall be subject to any form of finance or credit agreement, hire purchase or loan in the name of one party shall (be) (be deemed to be) the property of the party liable under the Agreement

4. Provision for specific items to be dealt with separately

If there should be particular items within Clause 3 above which the parties wish to own jointly such items shall be listed on a Schedule and signed by both parties and thereafter they shall be considered to be owned jointly

OR

If there should be particular items within Clause 3 above which the parties agree shall be owned by one of them alone such items shall be listed on a Schedule and signed by both parties and thereafter they shall be considered to be owned by that party

NOTE: See note agreement 1 clause 12

5. Items acquired on credit

By one party

(1) All items acquired by one party before or during the period of cohabitation and which are subject to any form of finance or credit agreement, hire purchase or loan shall (be) (be deemed to be) the property of the party liable under the finance or credit agreement, hire purchase or loan and that party shall be responsible for making all the repayments

Jointly

(2) All items acquired jointly before or during the period of cohabitation and which are subject to any form of finance or credit agreement, hire purchase or loan shall (be) (be deemed to be) the joint property of the parties and the parties shall be jointly responsible for making all the repayments.

NOTE: See note agreement 1 clause 13 (2)

Credit and loans

6. Joint bank loan, overdraft, credit card

All items costing over................pounds (£ ....) acquired either before or during the period of cohabitation the purchase of which is financed by a joint bank loan or overdraft facility, joint credit card or credit card in the sole name of one party and of which the other party is an authorised user or any other joint credit facility shall be considered to be owned jointly.

NOTE: See note agreement 1 clause 14

7. Credit cards

Sole Name

(1) All payments made pursuant to any credit card agreement or other finance or revolving credit agreement or loan facility (other than Mortgage repayments and as provided in Clause 5 above) which is in the sole name of one party shall be made [by that party] [equally] [as to *number* % by *A* and as to *number* % by *B*]

Joint/Authorised User

(2) All payments made pursuant to any credit card agreement or other finance or revolving credit agreement or loan facility (other than Mortgage repayments and as provided in Clause 5 above) which is in the joint names of the parties or a credit card agreement in the sole name of one party which the other party is an authorised user shall be made [equally] [as to *number* % by *A* and as to *number* % by *B*] [by *name* alone]

NOTE: See note agreement 1 clause 15

8. Family Loans

Joint Liability

(1) Any existing or future loans received from the family of either party shall be considered to be the joint liability of the parties and repayment shall be made [equally] [as to *number* % by *A* and as to *number* % by *B*] [by *name* alone]

OR

Sole Liability

(1) Any existing or future loans received from the family of either party shall be considered to be the sole liability of *[name]* and repayments shall be made [equally] [as to *number* % by *A* and as to *number* % by *B*] [by *name* alone]

Existing Loans

(2) The parties declare that [they have] *[name]* [has] received a loan of £............from *[name of lender]* repayable [on demand][by *[number]* instalments payable [monthly in advance][monthly in arrear]][interest-free][subject to interest of......% per cent per annum]

NOTE: See note agreement 1 clause 16

Other assets

9. Bank and Building Society Accounts (and other capital assets)

Joint

(1) Any joint Bank or Building Society account the parties have or may establish whether for the purpose of paying the expenses hereinbefore referred to or for any other purpose and any other jointly owned investment or capital asset (excluding the Home and Contents as hereinbefore defined and motor vehicles) shall belong to the parties [in equal shares] [as to *number* % to *A* and as to *number* % to *B*] irrespective of the proportions in which they contributed to the account or investment or acquisition of the asset.

AND

Sole

(2) Any Bank or Building Society account and any other investment or capital asset (excluding the Home and Contents as hereinbefore defined and motor vehicles) in the sole name of either party shall remain the property of that party

NOTE: See note agreement 1 clause 17

Pensions

10. Nominations

The parties will each nominate the other to receive [the whole] [*number* %] of the death in service benefits pension and/or other payments due under any pension scheme or schemes of which he or she may from time to time be a member.

11. Cancellation or Alteration of Nominations

Except on termination or variation of this Agreement any nomination made under the provisions of Clause 10 hereof shall not be cancelled or altered save with the prior written consent of the other party.

Children

12. Provisions for payment if child born

Fixed period

In the event of the parties suffering a reduction in income as a result of *[name]* having a child by *[name]* he shall pay all the expenses hereinbefore referred to for *[number]* months

OR

Agreed period

In the event of the parties suffering a reduction in income as a result of *[name]* having a child by *[name]* he shall pay all the expenses hereinbefore referred to for such period as shall be agreed between them

13. Maintenance Payable

Sole

Maintenance payable to or for a child or children of a previous relationship of one party by that party shall be paid by that party

OR

Joint

Maintenance payable to or for a child or children of a previous relationship of one party by that party shall be treated as part of common household expenditure referred to in Clause 2 above and shall be paid accordingly

14. Maintenance Received

Maintenance received for a child or children of a previous relationship of one party shall be used for the benefit of that child or children.

Disputes

15. *Dispute resolution*

If there should be any dispute between the parties concerning this agreement (other than disputes about valuation when the provisions for resolution of such disputes contained elsewhere in this agreement shall apply) either during the subsistence of this agreement or upon termination hereof which the parties are not able to resolve themselves, they agree to refer such dispute to [mutually convenient mediators of the Family Mediators Association] [a mutually convenient office of National Family Mediation] whilst reserving the right to refer the matter to the Court for adjudication if resolution of the dispute should not prove possible.

Termination/variation

16. *Termination*

This Agreement shall terminate on the happening of any of the following:

(a) The death of either party

(b) The marriage of the parties to each other

(c) Notice in writing given by one party to the other whereupon the transitional provisions below shall apply

(d) The parties agreeing mutually to cease to leave together whereupon the transitional provisions below shall apply

(e) The abandonment of the Home by one party and such abandonment being deemed by the other party to terminate the relationship whereupon the transitional provisions below shall apply

17. *Transitional provisions*

In the event of this Agreement being terminated except by death or marriage of the parties to each other, the following transitional provisions shall apply:

(1) If both parties wish to remain in the premises rented in joint names preference will be given to the party with whom any children will reside. If there are no children and the parties cannot agree who is to remain then they shall both vacate the premises

(2) Common household expenditure including any of the items as identified in Clause 2 hereof accruing from the date of separation until the transfer of the Home into the sole name of one party shall be paid by the party remaining in occupation

NOTE: See note agreement 1 clause 25 (8)

(3) Any Contents and motor vehicles and any Bank or Building Society accounts or other capital assets owned jointly shall be divided equally by agreement between the parties and in default of agreement shall be sold and realised and the proceeds divided equally

NOTE: See note agreement 1 clause 25(9).

(4) The parties shall take immediate steps to terminate the use of any credit card agreement or other finance or revolving credit agreement in the joint names of the parties or in the sole name of one party where the other party is an authorised user and whether or not such agreement has been terminated the parties shall be liable for the balance due under such agreement together with accrued interest in the proportions in which they made payments under Clause 7. If either party should obtain further credit after the date of separation that party shall remain solely liable for repayment together with accrued interest

Repayments as agreement

(5) Any loans from the family of either party outstanding at the date of termination shall continue to be repaid in accordance with Clause 8 above

OR

Repayments within family

(5) Any loans from the family of either party outstanding at the date of termination shall be repaid by the party from whose family the loan was received

(6) *A* and/or *B* shall pay maintenance to any child or children of the relationship at a rate to be agreed between the parties until the said child or children attain[s] the age of 17 years or if later cease[s] full time education and/or training

NOTE: Any such agreement would be subject to a Child Support Agency assessment.

(7) Any nomination or nominations in respect of any pension scheme or schemes made by either party under Clause 16 hereof shall be deemed to have been cancelled as from the date of termination

NOTE: Couples should be advised to take all necessary steps to notify pension fund administrators that such nominations are to be cancelled.

18. Variation

Any variation of this Agreement shall only be effective if recorded in a supplemental written Agreement executed by both parties.

IN WITNESS whereof the parties hereto have hereunto set their hands the day and year first before written

SCHEDULE

Contents

It is hereby agreed that notwithstanding the Contents clause herein the following items shall be considered to be owned by *[name]*

[LIST]

SIGNED AS A DEED
by the said

in the presence of

SIGNED AS A DEED
by the said

in the presence of

LIVING TOGETHER AGREEMENT 3: ONE PARTY TO RETAIN THE WHOLE OF BENEFICIAL INTEREST IN HOME

NOTE: Because of the likelihood that this agreement may be more advantageous to one party than to the other it may be that the parties should be advised to have separate legal representation

THIS DEED OF AGREEMENT is made the .... day of .... 19.....

BETWEEN:

1. *[name* ....*]* of *[address*...*]* ("*[A]*") and

2. *[name* ....*]* of *[address*...*]* ("*[B]*")

WHEREAS:

(1) The parties [live together] [intend to live together]

(2) The parties wish to enter into an agreement regulating their rights and obligations towards each other and towards any children of the relationship and of any previous relationship

(3) The parties intend that this Agreement shall be legally binding on them

(4) The parties declare that they have each had the benefit of independent legal advice prior to the execution of this agreement and are signing it voluntarily and in full understanding of their respective rights and liabilities hereunder.

OR

(4) The parties declare that they have been advised to seek independent legal advice but have declined to do so.

(5) The parties presently have no children

OR

(5) The parties presently have *[number]* child[ren] namely:-

(a) *[name(s)..............]* being the child[ren] of the relationship [of whom *[number]* are] presently under the age of majority

(b) *A* has *[number]* child[ren] namely *[name(s)..............]* being the child[ren] of a previous relationship [of whom *[number]* children are] presently under the age of majority

(c) *B* has *[number]* child[ren] namely *[name(s).............]* being the child[ren] of a previous relationship [of whom *[number]* are] presently under the age of majority

The Home

Existing Home

(6) The parties are presently resident at the address given above ("the Home") which is a property purchased in the sole name of *[name.............................]*

OR

Home to be purchased

(6) The parties are presently resident at the address[es] given above but intend to purchase a property ("the Home") in the sole name of *[name of owning party]* the address of which is *[address of the property to be purchased]*

IT IS HEREBY AGREED as follows:

The Home

1. The Home

(1) The Home [is] [will be] vested in the sole name of *[name of owning party]* and notwithstanding any contribution which *[name of non owning party]* may make directly or indirectly towards the purchase maintenance or improvement of the home [he][she] has and will acquire no beneficial interest whatsoever in the home

(2) From the date of this agreement *[name of owning party]* as licensor permits *[name of non-owning party]* to occupy the Home with [him][her] as licensee. This licence is personal to *[name of non-owning party]* and cannot be assigned. The licence shall determine upon reasonable notice or at the latest on completion of any sale of the Home and *[name of non-owning party]* shall vacate the Home and remove all [his][her] belongings on or before that date

NOTE: Where only one party owns the Home the other party has little or no security and it is appropriate for the owning party to grant a contractual licence to occupy to the non-owning party. This will ensure the right of the non-owning party to receive a reasonable period of notice if the relationship breaks down. It also enables the owning party to receive monetary contributions while minimising the risk that these will be construed as contributions towards the mortgage repayments.

It is possible to have a separate document and there are a number of existing precedents for contractual licences. However, they seem more suitable for a commercial and less personal type of arrangement such as students or friends sharing a house. The necessary provisions have therefore been incorporated in this precedent.

Outgoings

2. Outgoings

Common household expenditure including Council Tax or other local tax water rates, gas, electricity, telephone, television licence and/or rental agreement, buildings household and contents insurance, food, decorating and repairs costing less than £1,000 shall be paid [equally] [as to *number* % by *A* and as to *number* % by *B*] [by *name* alone]. [This provision shall also apply to payments of ground rent service charge(s) insurance premiums and any other sums due under the terms of any Lease by virtue of which the parties occupy the home]

NOTE: See note agreement 1 clause 9.

OR

2. *[Name of non-owning party]* will pay to *[name of owning party]* the sum of £........... per [week][calendar month] payable in advance on the first day of each [week][month] as a

contribution towards the common household expenditure. This sum may be varied by agreement between the parties.

Contents

3. Ownership of Contents Options

Sole

(1) All items of personal use or adornment shall belong to the party who last acquired them whether by inheritance gift or purchase and where the acquisition of any such item was financed by a credit facility in the name of the other party or in the joint names of the parties it shall nonetheless be considered to be solely the property of the party acquiring it and the subsequent provisions of this Agreement shall have no effect as regards items of personal use or adornment

Joint

(2) Subject to Clause 4, 5 and 6 below and except as may be specified in the Schedule hereto all furniture household garden or garage articles or effects and electrical equipment ("the Contents") shall be considered to be owned jointly regardless of when or by whom they were acquired

OR

Belong to party who acquired them

(2) Subject to Clauses 4, 5 and 6 below and except as may be specified in the Schedule hereto all furniture household garden or garage articles or effects and electrical equipment ("the Contents") shall belong to the party who last acquired them whether by inheritance gift or purchase

OR

All items costing over £..................belong to person who acquired them

(2) Subject to Clauses 4, 5 and 6 below and except as may be specified in the Schedule hereto all furniture household garden or garage articles or effects and electrical equipment ("the Contents") shall if worth over................pounds (£................) at the date of termination of this Agreement belong to the party who last acquired them whether by inheritance gift or purchase and all other items shall be considered to be owned jointly

Motor Vehicle – sole

(3) Any motor vehicle shall belong to the party who acquired it

OR

Motor Vehicle – joint

(3) Any motor vehicle shall be considered to be owned jointly regardless of when or by whom it was acquired except that any motor vehicle which at the date of termination of this Agreement shall be subject to any form of finance or credit agreement hire purchase or loan in the name of one party shall (be)(be deemed to be) the property of the party liable under the Agreement

4. Provision for specific items to be dealt with separately

If there should be particular items within Clause 3 above which the parties wish to own jointly such items shall be listed on the Schedule and signed by both parties and thereafter they shall be considered to be owned jointly

OR

If there should be particular items within Clause 3 above which the parties agree shall be owned by one of them alone such items shall be listed on a Schedule and signed by both parties and thereafter they shall be considered to be owned by that party

NOTE: See note agreement 1 clause 12

5. Items acquired on Credit

By one party

(1) All items acquired by one party before or during the period of cohabitation and which are subject to any form of finance or credit agreement hire purchase or loan shall [be][be deemed to be] the property of the party liable under the finance or credit agreement hire purchase or loan and that party shall be responsible for making all the repayments

NOTE: See note agreement 1 clause 13 (1)

Joint

(2) All items acquired jointly before or during the period of cohabitation and which are subject to any form of finance or credit agreement hire purchase or loan shall [be][be deemed to be] the joint property of the parties and the parties shall be jointly responsible for making all the repayments

NOTE: See note agreement 1 clause 13

Credit and loans

6. Joint Bank Loan, Overdraft, Credit Card

All items costing over................pounds (£ ....) acquired either before or during the period of cohabitation the purchase of which is financed by a joint bank loan or overdraft facility joint credit card or credit card in the sole name of one party and of which the other party is authorised user or any other joint credit facility shall be considered to be owned jointly

NOTE: See note agreement 1 clause 14

7. Credit Cards

Sole Name

(1) All payments made pursuant to any credit card agreement or other finance or revolving credit agreement or loan facility (other than Mortgage repayments and as provided in Clause 5 above) which is in the sole name of one party shall be made [by that party][equally][as to *number* % by *A* and as to *number* % by *B*]

Joint/Authorised User

(2) All payments made pursuant to any credit card agreement or other finance or revolving credit agreement or loan facility (other than Mortgage repayments and as provided in Clause 5 above) which is in the joint names of the parties or a credit card agreement in the sole name of one party of which the other party is an authorised user shall be made [equally][as to *number* % by *A* and as to *number* % by *B*] [by *name* alone]

NOTE: See note agreement 1 clause 15

8. Family Loans

Joint Liability

Any existing or future loans received from the family of either party shall be considered to be the joint liability of the parties and repayment shall be made [equally] [as to *number* % by *A* and as to *number* % by *B*] [by *name* alone]

OR

Sole Liability

(1) Any existing or future loans received from the family of either party shall be considered to be the sole liability of *[name]* and repayments shall be made [equally][as to *number* % by *A* and as to *number* % by *B*] [by *name* alone]

Existing Loans

(2) The parties declare that [they have]*[name]* [has] received a loan of £............from *[name of lender]* repayable [on demand][by *[number]* instalments payable [monthly in advance][monthly in arrear]] [interest-free][subject to interest of.............% per cent per annum]

NOTE: See note agreement 1 clause 16

Other assets

9. Bank and Building Society accounts (and other capital assets)

Joint

(1) Any joint Bank or Building Society account the parties may have or may establish whether for the purpose of paying the expenses hereinbefore referred to or for any other purpose and any other jointly owned investment or capital asset (excluding the Home and Contents as hereinbefore defined and motor vehicles) shall belong to the parties in equal shares irrespective of the proportions in which they contributed to the account or investment or acquisition of the asset

AND

Sole

(2) Any Bank or Building Society account and any other investment or capital asset (excluding the Home and Contents as hereinbefore defined and motor vehicles) in the sole name of either party shall remain the property of that party

NOTE: See note agreement 1 clause 17

Pensions

10. Nominations

The parties will each nominate the other to receive [the whole][*number* %] of the death in service benefits and pension and/or other payments due under any pension scheme or schemes of which he or she may from time to time be a member.

11. Cancellation or Alteration of Nominations

Except on termination or variation of this Agreement any nomination made under the provisions of Clause 10 hereof shall not be cancelled or altered save with the prior written consent of the other party.

Children

12 Provisions for payment if child born

Fixed period

In the event of the parties suffering a reduction in income as a result of *[name]* having a child by *[name]* he shall pay all the expenses hereinbefore referred to for *[number]* months

OR

Agreed period

In the event of the parties suffering a reduction in income as a result of *[name]* having a child by *[name]* he shall pay all the expenses hereinbefore referred to for such period as shall be agreed between them

13. Maintenance payable

Sole

Maintenance payable to or for a child or children of a previous relationship of one party by that party shall be paid by that party

OR

Joint

Maintenance payable to or for a child or children of a previous relationship of one party by that party shall be treated as part of common household expenditure referred to in Clause 2 above and shall be paid accordingly

14. Maintenance Received

Maintenance received for a child or children of a previous relationship of one party shall be used for the benefit of that child or children

Disputes

15. Dispute resolution

If there should be any dispute between the parties concerning this agreement (other than disputes about valuation when the provisions for resolution of such disputes contained elsewhere in this agreement shall apply) either during the subsistence of this agreement or upon termination hereof which the parties are not able to resolve themselves they agree to refer such dispute to [mutually convenient mediators of the Family Mediators Association] [a mutually convenient office of National Family Mediation] whilst reserving the right to refer the matter to the Court for adjudication if resolution of the dispute should not prove possible.

Termination/variation

16. Termination

This Agreement shall terminate on the happening of any of the following:

(a) The death of either party

(b) The marriage of the parties to each other

(c) Notice in writing given by one party to the other whereupon the transitional provisions below shall apply

(d) The parties agreeing mutually to cease to live together whereupon the transitional provisions below shall apply

(e) The abandonment of the home by one party and such abandonment being deemed by the other party to terminate the relationship whereupon the transitional provisions below shall apply

17. Transitional provisions

In the event of this Agreement being terminated except by death or marriage of the parties to each other, the following transitional provisions shall apply:

(1) *[Name of non-owning party]*'s licence to occupy shall determine and [he][she] shall vacate the Home and remove all [his][her] belongings within *[insert number of days]* from the date of termination of the agreement or the death of *[name of owning party]*

(2) *[Name of non-owning party]* shall be entitled to a refund of that proportion of the [weekly][monthly] contribution already paid in respect of any period after [he][she] vacates the Home

(3) Any Contents and motor vehicles and any Bank or Building Society accounts or other capital assets owned jointly shall be divided equally by agreement between the parties and in default of agreement shall be sold and realised and the proceeds divided equally

NOTE: See note agreement 1 clause 25 (9)

(4) The parties shall take immediate steps to terminate the use of any credit card agreement or other finance or revolving credit agreement in the joint names of the parties or in the sole name of one party where the other party is an authorised user and whether or not such agreement has been terminated the parties shall be liable for the balance due under such agreement together with accrued interest in the proportions in which they made payments under Clause 7. If either party should obtain further credit after the date of separation that party shall remain solely liable for repayment together with accrued interest

Repayments as agreement

(5) Any loans from the family of either party outstanding at the date of termination shall continue to be repaid in accordance with Clause 8 above

OR

Repayments within family

(6) Any loans from the family of either party outstanding at the date of termination shall be repaid by the party from whose family the loan was received

(7) *A* and/or *B* shall pay maintenance to any child or children of the relationship at a rate to be agreed between the parties until the said child or children attain[s] the age of 17 years or if later cease[s] full time education and/or training

NOTE: Any such agreement would be subject to a Child Support Agency assessment.

(8) Any nomination or nominations in respect of any pension scheme or schemes made by either party under Clause 10 hereof shall be deemed to have been cancelled as from the date of termination

NOTE: Couples should be advised to take all necessary steps to notify pension fund administrators that such nominations are to be cancelled.

18. Variation

Any variation of this Agreement shall only be effective if recorded in a supplemental written Agreement executed by both parties.

IN WITNESS WHEREOF the parties hereto have hereunto set their hands the day and year first before written

SCHEDULE

Contents

It is hereby agreed that notwithstanding the Contents clause herein the following items shall be considered to be owned by *[name]*

[LIST]

SIGNED AS A DEED
by the said
in the presence of

SIGNED AS A DEED
by the said
in the presence of

B.
DEEDS OF TRUST

DEED OF TRUST 1: PROPERTY IN JOINT NAMES

THIS DEED OF TRUST is made the..day of ....19......

BETWEEN:

1. *[name* ....*]* of *[address*..*]* ("*[A]*") and

2. *[name* ....*]* of *[address*..*]* ("*[B]*") and

3. *A* and *B* ("the Trustees")

WHEREAS:

(1) By a [Transfer] [Conveyance] [dated ....] [of even date but executed before this Deed] and made between *[name of Vendor]* ("the Vendor") of the one part and the Trustees of the other part and in consideration of the payment of the sum of .... pounds (£........................) the property described in the Schedule hereto ("the Home") was [Transferred] [Conveyed] to the Trustees in fee simple upon trust as therein stated

OR

(1) By a Lease [dated...................................] [of even date but executed before this Deed] and made between *[parties]* ("the Lease") the property described in the Schedule hereto ("the Home") was demised to [the Trustees] *[original lessee]* for the term of [...............] years from *[date]* at the yearly rent of £ .... subject to the terms and conditions of the Lease

[By an assignment [dated ....] [of even date but executed before this Deed] and made between *[assignor]* of the one part and the Trustees of the other part the Home is now vested in the Trustees for all the residue of the term of years granted by the Lease]

(2) By a Mortgage ("the Mortgage") [dated.....................................] [of even date] the Trustees charged the Home with the payment to *[name of Mortgagee]* as Mortgagees of the sum of..................pounds (£..........................) with interest thereon and subject to the terms and conditions of the Mortgage

Beneficial interest

Option A: Joint Tenants

(3) The parties have agreed that they are entitled to the beneficial interest in the Home as joint tenants in equity

OR

Option B: Equal Shares

(3) The parties have agreed that they are entitled to the beneficial interest in the Home in equal shares (This shall be the case regardless of the parties' respective contributions to the purchase price of the Home)

OR

Option C: % Shares

(3) The parties have agreed that they are entitled to the beneficial interest in the Home as to *[number]* % to *A* and as to *[number]* % to *B*. (This shall be the case regardless of the parties' respective contributions to the purchase price of the Home)

OR

Option D: Shares in Proportion to Purchase Price/Mortgage

(3) The parties have agreed that they are entitled to the beneficial interest in the Home in the proportions ("the agreed proportions") in which they contribute to the purchase of the Home whether by way of payment of mortgage instalments and mortgage linked endowment policy premiums as set out in Clause 1 and/or by way of future lump sum payment as set out in Clauses 2 and 4 of the Living Together Agreement [dated................] [of even date] entered into by the parties ("the Agreement")

OR

Option E: Provision for previous contributions by one or both parties to be taken into account. Remainder in accordance with Agreement or in stated shares

(3) The parties have agreed that they shall be entitled to the beneficial interest in the Home in proportions ("the agreed proportions") calculated on the basis that:

(a) *A* is entitled to a sum equal to *[number]* % of the sale price before deductions or ....pounds (£..) whichever is the greater as a result of having paid....................pounds (£..................)

AND/OR

B is entitled to a sum equal to *[number]* % of the sale price before deductions or ....pounds (£..) whichever is the greater as a result of having paid ....pounds..........(£..........)

AND/OR

[name] is entitled to a sum equal to *[number]*% of the sale price before deductions or ....pounds (£...........) whichever is the greater as a result of having obtained a discount in the purchase price due to [his][her] prior occupation of the Home as a tenant.

AND/OR

[name] is entitled to a sum equal to *[number]* % of the sale price before deductions or....................pounds (£................................) whichever is the greater as a result of having obtained a reduction in the purchase price as a benefit from [his][her] family

(b) The remainder shall be held in the proportions in which they contribute to the purchase of the Home whether by way of payment of mortgage instalments and mortgage linked endowment policy premiums as set out in Clause 1 and/or by way of future lump sum payment as set out in Clauses 2 and 4 of the Living Together Agreement [dated..............] [of even date] entered into by the parties ("the Agreement")

OR

(b) The remainder shall be held as to *[number]* % for *A* and as to *[number]* % for *B*

NOW THIS DEED WITNESSETH as follows:

1. The Trustees shall hold the Home on trust to sell the same with power to postpone the sale and shall hold the net rents and profits until sale and the net proceeds of sale (after deducting the balance of any monies due under the Mortgage) for themselves

Option A: joint tenants
as joint tenants in equity

Option B: equal shares
as tenants in common in equal shares

Option C: percentage shares
as tenants in common as to *[number]* % for *A* and as to *[number]* % for *B*

Options D and E: contributions/agreed proportions
as tenants in common in the agreed proportions

2. *A* and *B* HEREBY COVENANT with each other:

(a) To observe and perform all covenants restrictions conditions and stipulations at any time affecting the Home and the terms and conditions of the Mortgage [and of the Lease]

(b) To keep the Home and Contents insured against all usual comprehensive risks to the full reinstatement or replacement value of the same and to pay the insurance premiums in accordance with the terms of [the said Agreement] [the Living Together Agreement [dated...............] [of even date] entered into by *A* and *B* ("the Agreement")] and subject to the provisions of the Mortgage [and of the Lease] to apply any monies received on any policy of insurance effected on the home and contents in the replacement or reinstatement thereof

(c) That neither party shall create or purport to create any charge mortgage lien or other interest (other than the Mortgage) in respect of the Home as a whole or their respective shares or to dispose by sale gift or otherwise of the whole or part of their respective shares without the consent in writing of the other party

[except that this provision shall not restrict the right of either party to dispose of his or her share by Will]

NOTE: This alternative should be used if the parties hold the beneficial interest as tenants in common.

OR

[For the avoidance of doubt the parties declare that this provision shall not restrict the right of either to sever the equitable joint tenancy and subject thereto to dispose of his or her share by Will]

NOTE: This alternative should be used if the parties hold the beneficial interest as joint tenants.

(d) As between the parties the payment of monies due under the terms of the Mortgage [and of the Lease] and the funding of major repairs and improvements to the Home shall be as contained in the Agreement.

3. If either *A* or *B* (or their Personal Representatives) shall wish the Trust for sale to take effect he or she shall give notice to the other party in accordance with the terms of the Agreement and the

provisions as to the right of the other party to purchase the whole of the Home and the manner of any sale shall be as contained in the Agreement

4. On completion of the sale of the Home (other than by way of purchase by one party of the other's share) the proceeds after deduction of all sums repayable under the Mortgage [outstanding under the Lease] and all expenses of sale shall belong to *A* and *B* in the proportions stated in Clause 1 above

IN WITNESS whereof the parties hereto have hereunto set their hands the day and year first before written

SCHEDULE

SIGNED AS A DEED
by the said

in the presence of

SIGNED AS A DEED
by the said

in the presence of

DEED OF TRUST 2: PROPERTY IN SOLE NAME

THIS DEED OF TRUST is made the.. day of ....19........

BETWEEN:

1. *[name* ....*]* of *[address* ....*]* ("the Owner") and

2. *the Owner and [name*...*]*

of *[address*..*]* ("the Beneficial Owners")

WHEREAS:

(1) By a [Transfer] [Conveyance] [dated ....] [of even date but executed before this Deed] and made between *[name of Vendor* ....*]* ("the Vendor") of the one part and the Owner of the other part and in consideration of the payment of the sum of...............pounds (£..................................) the property described in the Schedule hereto ("the Home") was [Transferred] [Conveyed] to the Owner in fee simple

OR

(1) By a Lease [dated ....] [of even date but executed before this Deed] and made between *[parties]* ("the Lease") the property described in the Schedule hereto ("the Home") was demised to [the Owner] *[the original lessee]* for the term of [..................] years from *[date]* at the yearly rent of £................................ subject to the terms and conditions of the Lease

[By an Assignment [dated...............................] [of even date but executed before this Deed] and made between *[assignor]* of the one part and the Owner of the other part the Home is now vested in the Owner for all the residue of the term of years granted by the Lease]

(2) By a Mortgage ("the Mortgage") [dated......................................] [of even date] the Owner charged the Home with the payment to *[name of Mortgagee]* as Mortgagees of the sum of..............pounds (£....................................) with interest thereon and subject to the terms and conditions of the Mortgage

(3) The Owner is desirous of transferring the benefit of ownership in the Home to the Beneficial Owners so that the net proceeds of sale shall belong as from the date hereof to the Beneficial Owners as hereinafter stated

NOW THIS DEED WITNESSETH as follows:

1. The Owner HEREBY DECLARES that [he][she] holds the Home on trust for the Beneficial Owners and hereby agrees that [he][she] will at the request and cost of the Beneficial Owners [transfer or convey] [assign] the same to such person or persons at such time or times and in such manner or otherwise deal with the same as the Beneficial Owners shall direct

2. The Beneficial Owners HEREBY COVENANT with each other:

(a) To observe and perform all covenants restrictions conditions and stipulations at any time affecting the Home and the terms and conditions of the Mortgage [and of the Lease]

(b) To keep the Home and Contents insured against all usual comprehensive risks to the full reinstatement or replacement value of the same and to pay the insurance premiums in accordance with the terms of the Living Together Agreement [dated ....] [of even date] entered into by the Beneficial Owners ("the Agreement") and subject to the provisions of the Mortgage [and of the Lease] to apply any monies received on any policy of insurance effected on the Home and Contents in the replacement or reinstatement thereof

(c) That neither party shall create or purport to create any charge, mortgage lien or other interest (other than the Mortgage) in respect of the Home as a whole or their respective shares or to dispose by sale gift or otherwise of the whole or part of their respective shares without the consent in writing of the other party

[except that this provision shall not restrict the right of either party to dispose of his or her share by Will]

NOTE: See note deed of trust 1 clause 2 (c).

OR

[For the avoidance of doubt the parties declare that this provision shall not restrict the right of either to sever the equitable joint tenancy and subject thereto to dispose of [his][her] share by Will]

NOTE: See note deed of trust 1 clause 2 (c).

(d) As between the parties the payment of monies due under the terms of the Mortgage [and of the Lease] and the funding of major repairs and improvements to the Home shall be as contained in the Agreement.

3. If either *A* or *B* (or their Personal Representatives) shall wish the Home to be sold [he][she] shall give notice to the other party in accordance with the terms of the Agreement and the provisions as to the right of the other party to purchase the whole of the Home and the manner of any sale shall be as contained in the Agreement

4. On completion of the sale of the Home (other than by way of purchase by one party of the other party's share) the proceeds of sale after deduction of all sums repayable under the Mortgage [outstanding under the Lease] and all expenses of sale shall belong to *A* and *B*

Option A: Joint Tenants

as joint tenants in equity

OR

Option B: Equal Shares

in equal shares (which shall be the case regardless of the parties' respective contributions to the purchase price of the Home)

OR

Option C: % Shares

as to *[number]* % for *A* and as to *[number]* % for *B* (which shall be the case regardless of the parties' respective contributions to the purchase price of the Home)

OR

Option D: Contributions

in the proportions in which they contribute to the purchase of the Home whether by way of payment of mortgage instalments and mortgage linked endowment premiums as set out in Clause 1 and/or by way of lump sum payment as set out in Clauses 2 and 4 of the Agreement

OR

Option E: Agreed Proportions

(a) in proportions calculated on the basis that:

A is entitled to a sum equal to *[number]* % of the sale price before deductions or ....pounds (£..........................) whichever is the greater as a result of having paid................................pounds (£...)

AND/OR

B is entitled to a sum equal to *[number]* % of the sale price before deductions or ....pounds (£.........................) whichever is the greater as a result of having paid.................................pounds (£...)

AND/OR

[name] is entitled to a sum equal to *[number]* % of the sale price before deductions or ....pounds (£..................................) whichever is the greater as a result of having obtained a discount in the purchase price due to [his][her] prior occupation of the Home as a tenant

AND/OR

[name] is entitled to a sum equal to *[number]* % of the sale price before deductions or ....pounds (£..) whichever is the greater as a result of having obtained a discount in the purchase price as a benefit from [his][her] family

(b) and the remainder in the proportions in which they contribute to the purchase of the Home whether by way of payment of mortgage instalments and mortgage linked endowment policy premiums as set out in Clause 1 and/or by way of future lump sum payment as set out in Clauses 2 and 4 of the Agreement

OR

(b) and the remainder as to *[number]* % for *A* and as to *[number]* % for *B*

OR

Option F: Sole Name. That party to have benefit of value to date. Remainder in accordance with agreement

on the basis that *[name of non-owner]* is not entitled to any beneficial interest in the Home as at the date of this Deed. The agreed value of the Home less the amount outstanding on the Mortgage as at the date hereof is.................pounds (£..) and *[owner]* shall be entitled to this sum out of the net proceeds of sale before division and in addition to any further share to which [he][she] may become entitled under the terms of the Agreement. From the date hereof *[non-owner]* shall acquire a beneficial interest and hereafter the parties shall be entitled to the beneficial interest in the Home in the proportions in which they contribute to the purchase of the Home whether by way of payment of mortgage instalments and mortgage linked endowment policy premiums as set out in Clause 1 and/or by way of future lump sum payment as set out in Clauses 2 and 4 of the Agreement

OR

Option G: Sole Name. That party to have benefit of value at date of commencement of cohabitation. Remainder in accordance with agreement

on the basis that at the commencement of cohabitation on or about *[date] [name of non-owner]* had no beneficial interest in the Home. From the said date *[non-owner]* acquired a beneficial interest. The agreed value of the Home less the amount outstanding on the mortgage as at the said date was...............pounds (£....................) and *[owner]* shall be entitled to this sum out of the net proceeds of sale before division and in addition to any further share to which [he][she] may become entitled under the terms of the Agreement. From the date hereof (non-owner) shall acquire a beneficial interest and hereafter the parties shall be entitled to the beneficial interest in the Home in the proportions in which they contribute to the purchase of the Home whether by way of payment of Mortgage instalments and Mortgage Linked Endowment Policy Premiums as set out in Clause 1 and/or by way of future lump sum payment as set out in Clauses 2 and 4 of the Agreement

OR

Option H: Sole Name. That party to have benefit of value to date. Remainder in stated shares

on the basis that *[name of non-owner]* is not entitled to any beneficial interest in The Home as at the date of This Deed. The agreed value of the Home less the amount outstanding on the mortgage as at the date hereof is................pounds (£.......................................) and *[owner]* shall be entitled to this sum out of any net proceeds of sale before division and in addition to [his][her] percentage share in any increase in value in the Home over and above the said sum. The parties declare that they are entitled to the beneficial interest in any increase in the value of the Home over and above the said sum as to *[number]* % to *A* and as to *[number]* % to *B*

OR

Option I: Sole Name. That party to have benefit of value at date of commencement of cohabitation. Remainder in stated shares

on the basis that at the commencement of cohabitation on or about *[date] [name of non-owner]* had no beneficial interest in the Home. From the said date *[non-owner]* acquired a beneficial interest. The agreed value of the Home less the amount outstanding on the mortgage as at the commencement of cohabitation on or about *[date]* was................pounds (£........................) and *[owner]* shall be entitled to this sum out of the net proceeds of sale before division and in addition to [his][her] percentage share in any increase in value in the Home over and above the said sum. The parties declare that they are entitled to the beneficial interest in any increase in value of the Home over and above the said sum as to *[number]* % for *A* and as to *[number]* % for *B*

NOTE: See note agreement 1 recital 7 (F) to (I).

IN WITNESS whereof the parties hereto have hereunto set their hands the day and year first before written

SCHEDULE

SIGNED AS A DEED
by the said

in the presence of

SIGNED AS A DEED
by the said

in the presence of

SECTION 2

LIVING WITH THE ELDERLY

A.
AGREEMENTS

LIVING TOGETHER AGREEMENT 4: ALL PARTIES TO HAVE SHARE OF BENEFICIAL INTEREST IN HOME

NOTE: This precedent regulates the rights and obligations of an elderly person and a relative or couple with whom they will be sharing accommodation. It is not intended to regulate the rights and obligations of spouses or cohabiting partners as between themselves.

THIS DEED OF AGREEMENT is made the .... day of ....19......

BETWEEN:

1. *[name* ....*]* of *[address*...*]* ("*[A]*") and

2. *[name* ....*]* of *[address*...*]* ("*[B]*") and

3. *[name* ....*]* of *[address*...*]* ("[C]")

WHEREAS:

(1) The parties share [intend to share] the Home (as defined below)

(2) The parties wish to enter into an agreement regulating their rights and obligations towards each other

(3) The parties intend that this Agreement shall be legally binding on them

(4) The parties declare that they have each had the benefit of independent legal advice prior to the execution of this agreement and are signing it voluntarily and in full understanding of their respective rights and liabilities hereunder.

OR

The parties declare that they have been advised to seek independent legal advice but have declined to do so.

The Home – Legal Title

Legal Title – Existing Property

(5) *[Name(s)][is][are]* presently resident at *[address]* ("the Home") which is a property purchased [in the name(s) of...................] [in their joint names]

OR

Legal Title – Existing Property – to be transferred to all

(5) *[Names(s)...]*[is][are] presently resident at [address] ("the Home") which is a property purchased in the name(s) of................... but which it is intended to transfer into the names of all the parties

OR

Legal Title – Property to be Purchased

(5) The parties are presently resident at the address[es] given above but intend to purchase a property ("the Home") [in the name(s) of................] [in their joint names] the address of which is *[address of property to be purchased]*

The Home – Beneficial Interest

NOTE: It is suggested that in most cases people entering into this type of agreement will also execute a deed of trust setting out their respective beneficial interests in the home. This will of course be essential if the agreed beneficial interests are to be varied from the provisions in the conveyance/transfer of the property on purchase.

If a deed of trust is not to be executed then recital 6 will need to refer instead to the beneficial interests as contained in the conveyance/transfer of the property to the parties or to one or more of them.

(6) The parties intend to enter into a Deed of Trust which will provide as follows:

Option A: Joint Tenants

They [are] [shall be] entitled to the beneficial interest in the Home as joint tenants in equity.

OR

Option B: Joint Tenants and Tenants in Common

Regardless of their respective contributions to the purchase price of the Home they [are] [shall be] entitled to the beneficial interest in the Home as tenants in common as to *[number]* % to *A* and *B* which they shall hold as joint tenants in equity as between themselves and as to *[number]* % to *C*

OR

Option C: % Shares

Regardless of their respective contributions to the purchase price of the Home they [are] [shall be] entitled to the beneficial interest in the Home as to *[number]* % to *A* and as to *[number]* % to *B* and as to *[number]* % to *C*

OR

Option D: Shares in Proportion to Contributions to Purchase Price/Mortgage

They are and shall be entitled to the beneficial interest in the Home in the proportions in which they contribute to the purchase of the Home whether by way of payment of mortgage instalments as set out in Clause 1 and/or by way of future lump sum payment as set out in Clauses 2 and 4

OR

Option E: Provision for previous contributions by any party to be taken into account. Remainder in accordance with agreement or in stated shares

(a) From the date hereof they shall be entitled to the beneficial interest in the Home calculated on the basis that

A is entitled to a sum equal to *[number]* % of the sale price before deductions or.......... pounds (£................) whichever is the greater as a result of having paid £..................

AND/OR

B is entitled to a sum equal to *[number]* % of the sale price before deductions or................pounds (£...................) whichever is the greater as a result of having paid £.................

AND/OR

A and *B* are together entitled to a sum equal to *[number]* % of the sale price before deductions or...................pounds (£...........) whichever is the greater as a result of having paid £.............

AND/OR

C is entitled to a sum equal to *[number]* % of the sale price before deductions or................pounds (£..............) whichever is the greater as a result of having paid £................

AND/OR

[name(s)] [is][are] entitled to a sum equal to *[number]* % of the sale price before deductions or................pounds (£..............) whichever is the greater as a result of having obtained a discount in the purchase price due to [his][her][their] prior occupation of the Home as [a tenant][tenants]

AND/OR

[name] is entitled to a sum equal to *[number]* % of the sale price before deductions or...............pounds (£...................) whichever is the greater as a result of having obtained a discount in the purchase price as a benefit from [his][her] family

(b) and the remainder shall be held in the proportions in which they contribute to the purchase of the Home whether by way of payment of mortgage instalments set out in Clause 1 and/or by way of future lump sum payment as set out in Clauses 2 and 4

OR

(b) and the remainder as to *[number]* % for *A* and as to *[number]* % for *B* and as to *[number]* % for *C*

NOTE: Option E(a) records contributions made by one or more parties prior to the date of the agreement either by lump sum payment and/or discount under a "right to buy" tenancy or because of a reduction in the purchase price of a property purchased from a member of the family (e.g. where a parent has inherited a house he/she may agree a sale below market value).

Option E(b) allows alternative ways of dealing with the remainder of the equity. Extreme care needs to be taken when calculating the respective shares of the parties so as to take account of a lump sum payment and/or discount by one or more party(ies) as at the date of the agreement. If any party wishes to preserve a percentage it must be clearly shown whether such percentage is to be calculated by reference to the eventual sale price or to net proceeds after deductions including mortgage since otherwise there may be, at best, ambiguity and at worst an unintended result.

OR

(b) and the remainder shall be held as to *[number]* % for *A* and *B* which they shall hold as joint tenants in equity as between themselves and as to *[number]* % for *C*

OR

Option F: Benefit of Value to date. Remainder in accordance with this Agreement

[Name(s) of non-owning party(ies)] [is][are] not entitled to any beneficial interest as at the date of this Agreement. The agreed value of the Home less the amount outstanding on the mortgage as at the date hereof is...........pounds (£...............) and *[name(s) of owning party(ies)]* shall be entitled to this sum out of any net proceeds of sale before division and in addition to any further share to which [he][she][they] may become entitled under the terms of this Agreement. From the date of this Agreement *[name(s) of non-owning party(ies)]* shall acquire a beneficial interest and hereafter the parties shall be entitled to the beneficial interest in the proportions in which they contribute to the purchase of the Home whether by way of payment of mortgage instalments as set out in Clause 1 and/or by way of future lump sum payment as set out in Clauses 2 and 4

OR

Option G: Benefit of Value at date of Commencement of Sharing. Remainder in accordance with this Agreement

At the commencement of sharing on or about *[date] [name(s) of non-owning party(ies)]* had no beneficial interest in the Home. The agreed value of the Home less the amount outstanding on the mortgage as at the date was................pounds (£..............) and *[name(s) of owning party(ies)]* shall be entitled to this sum out of any net proceeds of sale before division and in addition to any further share to which [he][she][they] may become entitled under the terms of this Agreement. From the said date *[name(s) of non-owning party(ies)]* acquired a beneficial interest and the parties are and shall be entitled to the beneficial interest in the proportions in which they contribute to the purchase of the Home whether by way of payment of mortgage instalments as set out in Clause 1 and/or by way of future lump sum payment as set out in Clauses 2 and 4

OR

Option H: Benefit of Value to date. Remainder in stated shares

[Name(s) of non-owning party(ies)] [is][are] not entitled to any beneficial interest as at the date of this Agreement. The agreed value of the Home less the amount outstanding on the mortgage as at the date hereof is............pounds (£............) and *[name(s) of owning party(ies)]* shall be entitled to this sum out of any net proceeds of sale before division and in addition to [his][her][their] percentage share in any increase in the value of the Home over and above the said sum. The parties declare that from the date of this Agreement they are entitled to the beneficial interest in any increase in the value of the Home over and above the said sum [in equal shares] [as to *[number]* % to *A* and as to *[number]* % to *B* and as to *[number]* % to *C*] [as to *[number]* % to *A* and *B* and as to *[number]* % to *C* and *A* and *B* declare that they hold all their share and interest in the Home as beneficial joint tenants as between themselves]

OR

Option I: Benefit of Value at date of Commencement of Sharing. Remainder in stated shares

At the commencement of sharing on or about *[date] [name(s) of non-owning party(ies)]* had no beneficial interest in the Home. The agreed value of the Home less the amount outstanding on the mortgage at the commencement of sharing on or about *[date]* was............pounds (£............) and *[name(s) of owning party(ies)]* shall be entitled to this sum out of any net proceeds of sale before division and in addition to [his][her][their] percentage share in any increase in the value of the Home over and above the said sum. The parties declare that they are entitled to the beneficial interest in any increase in the value of the Home over and above the said sum [in equal shares] [as to *[number]* % to *A* as to *[number]* % to *B* and as to *[number]* % to

C] [as to *[number]* % to *A* and *B* and as to *[number]* % to *C* and *A* and *B* declare that they hold all their share and interest in the Home as beneficial joint tenants as between themselves]

NOTE: Options F to I deal with the situation where the property was in the name or names of one or more party(ies) prior to commencement of sharing and the value of the equity at that time is to be preserved for the original owner(s). The difference between F and G is to cater for the fact that the parties may be making this agreement when they commence sharing or some time later. The difference between F/G and H/I is to allow parties alternative ways of dealing with the equity from commencement of sharing onwards.

IT IS HEREBY AGREED as follows:

The Home

1. *Mortgage payment options*

% Payment

(1) The mortgage repayments shall be paid as to *[number]* % by *A* as to *[number]* % by *B* and as to *[number]* % by *C*

OR

Payment by some

(1) The mortgage repayments shall be paid by *[name(s)]* alone

NOTE: If the parties are to own the beneficial interest in the home in accordance with options D, E, F or G of clause 6 of the recitals, the percentage payments stated here will determine the proportions in which they are to be entitled to the beneficial interest (subject to the provisions dealing with future lump sum payments and improvements). Failure to pay will not affect this.

OR

Payment by agreement

(1) The mortgage repayments shall be paid as agreed from time to time between the parties SAVE that it is further agreed that the proportions in which they hold the beneficial interest in the Home shall be calculated by reference to the actual payments made by each

NOTE: This clause can be used if the parties wish the proportions in which they hold the beneficial interest to be calculated by reference to the actual payments made by each BUT it should be made clear that it would be necessary to keep careful and complete proof of such payments. If this option is chosen the sub clause (2) "Failure to pay" should be omitted.

Failure to pay

(2) If any party shall fail to pay [his][her] share of the mortgage for whatever reason and the other [party][parties] shall pay that share in addition to [his][her][their] own share then notwithstanding such failure to pay it is agreed that the respective shares of the parties in the beneficial interest in the Home shall remain unaltered

NOTE: Without the clause, if one party failed to pay his or her agreed share for whatever reason, the beneficial interest would be subject to change and could only be calculated in any subsequent dispute by extensive investigation of actual payments made by each party. The clause, therefore, provides certainty, but it should be made clear to the parties the position if one does not pay the agreed share.

2. *Capital payments in discharge of Mortgage*

Where any party makes a capital payment in discharge or part discharge of any mortgage secured on the Home that party's percentage share in the beneficial interest in the Home shall be adjusted to reflect such capital payment. The adjusted percentage shall be calculated by reference to the value of the Home at the time of such payment such value to be agreed between the parties and, if not so agreed, determined by a Valuer appointed jointly by the parties or in default by a Valuer to be appointed by the President for the time being of the Royal Institution of Chartered Surveyors. The particulars of such adjustments shall be recorded in accordance with the variation Clause

NOTE: It is important that any variation is recorded at the time such payment is made and the parties should be advised accordingly.

3. Negative Equity

(1) Where on any sale of the Home the liability remaining outstanding on the mortgage exceeds the proceeds of sale then in the absence of any written agreement to the contrary such liability shall be borne by the parties in the proportions in which they hold the beneficial interest in the Home.

(2) Where on any transfer of the Home from one party[ies] to the other[s] the liability remaining outstanding on the mortgage exceeds the value of the Home then in the absence of any written agreement to the contrary such deficit shall be borne by the parties in the proportions in which they hold the beneficial interest in the Home. The value of the Home shall be agreed between the parties and if not so agreed determined by a Valuer appointed jointly by the parties or in default by a Valuer to be appointed by the President for the time being of the Royal Institution of Chartered Surveyors.

NOTE: If one of Options E to I in the Recitals is chosen then it will be necessary for the parties to consider the effect of the Negative Equity clause and to decide their respective liabilities.

4. Improvements

Improvements which add to the value of the Home shall not be undertaken except by prior agreement between the parties. Where any party makes a contribution by payment for or part payment for such previously agreed improvements which increase the value of the Home that party's percentage share in the beneficial interest in the Home shall be adjusted to reflect such contribution. The increase in value and the adjusted percentage shall be calculated by reference to the value of the Home at the time of such payment such value to be agreed between the parties and, if not so agreed, determined by a Valuer to be appointed jointly by the parties and in default by a Valuer to be appointed by the President for the time being of the Royal Institution of Chartered Surveyors. The particulars of such adjustments shall be recorded in accordance with the variation Clause.

NOTE: The parties should be advised of the need to have the property valued at the time the improvement is made.

5. Non-monetary contributions

Where a party makes a non-monetary contribution which increases the value of the Home such a contribution shall not affect that party's beneficial interest in the Home unless the parties agree in advance that that party's share shall thereby be increased. The particulars of such agreed increase shall be recorded in accordance with the variation Clause.

NOTE: Because of the disparity in judgments in reported cases as to what amounts to a non-monetary contribution sufficient to affect the beneficial interest in the home, it is suggested that this clause be included by which the parties agree that such a non-monetary contribution shall not affect the beneficial interest of the party making the contribution unless they agree in advance that it should.

6. Major Repairs

(1) Any repair to the Home the cost of which will, or is likely to, exceed £1,000.00 shall not be undertaken except by prior agreement between the parties and if the cost does exceed that sum it shall be funded as agreed between the parties at the time the repair is undertaken and in default of such agreement it shall be funded [equally] [as to *[number]* % by *A* and as to *[number]* % by *B* and as to *[number]* % by *C*] [by name(s) alone]

(2) Contributions to the funding of any repairs to the Home shall not entitle the payer[s] to any share or increased share in the beneficial interest in the Home

(3) Where the parties agree at the time that a repair to the Home is undertaken that such repair is to be treated as an improvement then the provisions of Clause 4 shall apply in place of sub clause (1) and (2) above

NOTE: The figure of £1,000 is included as an example only and can be any figure chosen by the parties.

7. Replacement Home

(1) Where the parties acquire a property to replace the Home they shall enter into a declaration of trust at the time of purchase setting out their respective beneficial interests in the replacement home (the declaration to be contained in the Conveyance or Transfer or Lease or Assignment of the replacement home to the parties or any of them and/or to be contained in a separate Deed entered into by the parties)

(2) In default of any such Deed of Trust and in the absence of any express contrary provision in the said Conveyance Transfer Lease or Assignment the beneficial interest in the replacement home shall be held in the same proportions as the beneficial interest in the Home at the date of sale

NOTE: There have been cases where there was no express declaration of trust in the conveyance or transfer of the property as to the beneficial interest and this clause has been included to ensure that even in such a situation the beneficial interest is still clear.

Outgoings

8. Outgoings

Common household expenditure including Council Tax or other local tax, water rates, gas, electricity, telephone, television licence and/or rental agreement, buildings household and contents insurance, food, decorating and repairs costing less than £1,000.00 shall be paid [equally] [as to *number* % by *A* as to *number* % by *B* and as to *[number]* % by C] [by *[name]* alone]. [This provision shall also apply to payment of ground rent service charge(s) insurance premiums and any other sums due under the terms of any Lease by virtue of which the parties occupy the Home]

NOTE: This list is not exhaustive and can be amended to suit clients' individual requirements.

9. Arrangements for payment

The parties declare that notwithstanding the practical arrangements made by them as between themselves for actual payment in respect of the mortgage and common household expenditure their respective interests in the Home are as set out in Clause (6) of the recitals hereof

NOTE: The parties may, for practical reasons, decide to have separate accounts so that, for example, one makes all the mortgage payments and the other the common household expenses. This clause is to make it clear that such practical arrangements will not affect the beneficial interest.

Contents

10. Ownership of contents options

Personal items and household items

(1) All items of personal use or adornment and all furniture household garden or garage articles or effects and electrical equipment shall belong to the party[ies] who last acquired them whether by inheritance gift or purchase

NOTE: This Clause has been drafted on the assumption that the parties would not wish to own items jointly as between all of them. Items owned jointly by spouses or partners will be covered by this Clause.

OTHER CLAUSE OPTIONS

If the parties wish to include in the agreement clauses dealing with motor vehicles, items acquired on credit, bank loans, overdrafts, credit cards or family loans precedents for these can be found in Agreement 1.

Accounts

11. Bank and Building Society Accounts

Any joint Bank or Building Society account the parties may have or may establish in all their names for the purpose of paying the expenses hereinbefore referred to shall belong to the parties [in equal shares] [as to *[number]* % to *A* as to *[number]* % to *B* and as to *[number]* % to *C*] irrespective of the proportions in which they contributed to the account.

NOTE: Many people believe that joint bank accounts mean that the account holders are equally entitled to the money in the account. This is not true and in the absence of express agreement it could be difficult to justify who should have what. This can be particularly difficult if one party dies and banks have been known to freeze accounts leaving the survivors without access to any money.

Another aspect to consider is that if the elderly person wishes to have a son or daughter as joint holder or signatory on an account, ownership of the funds needs to be made clear at the outset, perhaps by notification to the bank or building society, to avoid any subsequent dispute particularly if the account forms part of the elderly person's estate on death.

Disputes

12. Dispute resolution

If there should be any dispute between the parties concerning this agreement (other than disputes about valuation when the provisions for resolution of such disputes contained elsewhere in this agreement shall apply) either during the subsistence of this agreement or upon termination hereof which the parties are not able to resolve themselves they agree to refer such dispute to mutually convenient mediators of the Family Mediators Association whilst reserving the right to refer the matter to the Court for adjudication if resolution of the dispute should not prove possible.

Termination/variation

13. Termination

This Agreement shall terminate on the happening of any of the following:

(a) The death of any party

(b) Notice in writing given by any party to the other[s] whereupon the transitional provisions below shall apply

(c) The parties agreeing mutually to cease to live together whereupon the transitional provisions below shall apply

(d) The abandonment of the home by any party and such abandonment being deemed by the other party[ies] to terminate the agreement whereupon the transitional provisions below shall apply. Abandonment shall not be deemed to terminate the agreement if the party[ies] remaining in occupation have actual or constructive knowledge of the abandoning [party's]-[parties'] whereabouts

14. Transitional Provisions

On termination of the agreement:-

(1) In the event of the death of any party and if neither of the surviving owners inherits the deceased owner's share of the beneficial interest in the Home ("the share") then they or either of them shall have the option to purchase the share upon the following terms:-

(a) the value of the Home shall be the value adopted by the deceased's Personal Representatives for probate purposes and the deceased's share of the Home shall be valued without reference to the joint ownership

(b) the option is personal to the surviving owners and shall be exercised by them or either of them during their lifetimes (subject to (c) below) and not by any person including their Personal Representatives after death

(c) any surviving owner wishing to exercise the option shall give notice to the Personal Representatives within two months from issue of the Grant of Representation to the deceased's estate and shall be given a further period of two months within which to complete the purchase of the deceased's share

NOTE: The parties should be advised to check the terms and status of any life policy which is intended to redeem a mortgage, as significantly different results will occur depending on whether or not the policy is assigned to the mortgagee or there is a notice of deposit. If the mortgage is automatically discharged the value of the beneficial interest is thereby increased for the benefit of all surviving owners. For example, if husband, wife and mother own the property jointly and there is a life policy on the husband's life or on the joint lives of husband and wife paying out on the first death, then if the husband dies ***and*** *the policy discharges the mortgage, both wife and mother will benefit which may not have been the intention. If the policy was not assigned to the mortgagee it will form part of the husband's estate unless it was written in trust. In that case, the mortgage debt will remain.*

(d) Upon exercising the option to purchase the deceased's share the surviving owner[s] shall be entitled to pay the purchase price to the deceased's estate by *[number]* equal instalments payable [monthly][quarterly][annually] [in advance][in arrear] [interest free][subject to interest of.....................per cent per annum]

(2) In the event of the agreement being terminated by notice in writing given by any party or parties to the other[s].-

(a) Unless otherwise agreed in writing *[name]* shall vacate the Home within four months from service of the notice or on completion of sale of the property if earlier

NOTE 1: The name to be inserted is to be decided by the parties when the agreement is being drawn up but they may wish to consider whether it should only be the original owner or owners who can require the other party or parties to vacate.

NOTE 2: This does not affect the statutory or common law rights as between the parties to obtain possession of the property or an injunction.

(b) Any party[ies] remaining in the Home shall be given a period of four months from the termination of the Agreement within which to complete the purchase of the other [party's][parties'] interest in the Home

NOTE: A period of four months was inserted as being the minimum reasonable period by which one party could make all the necessary financing arrangements to complete the purchase of the others interest whilst ensuring that the matter does not drag on for too long. However an alternative period can be inserted.

If the parties require a Clause for payment by instalments, Clause 14(1)(d) can be adapted. While there would be advantages to the parties remaining in occupation in having the instalment option, it could cause hardship to the party leaving who would have to vacate at the end of the notice period but might not receive full payment for several years.

(3) The purchasing party[ies] shall take all necessary steps to obtain the release of the selling party[ies] from all liability under the existing Mortgage[s] (if any)

(4) The value of the Home shall be the fair market value with vacant possession (and each party's share shall be valued proportionately without reference to the joint ownership) placed upon it by a Valuer agreed between the parties and in default appointed by the President for the time being of the Royal Institution of Chartered Surveyors

(5) If no party is to remain in the Home, or if any party wishing to remain in the Home is unable to complete the purchase within the specified period, the Home shall be sold for the best price reasonably obtainable as agreed between the parties or certified by the selling agent and in default by a Valuer appointed by the President for the time being of the Royal Institution of Chartered Surveyors and the net proceeds shall be divided between the parties in accordance with their beneficial interests as hereinbefore provided

Mortgage payments as agreement

(6) Until sale or transfer of the Home, the Mortgage shall continue to be paid as set out in Clause 1 above

OR

Mortgage payments by occupier

(6) Until sale or transfer of the Home, the mortgage shall be paid by the party[ies] remaining in occupation until sale or transfer credit being given for payment over and above [his][her][their] share.

(7) Common household expenditure including any of the items as identified in Clause 8 hereof accruing from the date [name(s)] vacate the Home until sale or transfer into the name[s] of the party[ies] remaining in occupation shall be paid by them.

15. *Variation*

Any variation of this Agreement and any adjustment in the respective shares of the parties in the beneficial interest in the Home pursuant to Clauses 2, 4 and 5 shall only be effective if recorded in a supplemental written agreement executed by all parties.

IN WITNESS whereof the parties hereto have hereunto set their hands the day and year first before written

SIGNED AS A DEED
by the said

in the presence of

SIGNED AS A DEED
by the said

in the presence of

SIGNED AS A DEED
by the said

in the presence of

LIVING TOGETHER AGREEMENT 5: ONE PARTY OR MORE TO RETAIN THE WHOLE OF BENEFICIAL INTEREST IN HOME

This precedent regulates the rights and obligations of an elderly person and a relative or couple with whom they will be sharing accommodation. It is not intended to regulate the rights and obligations of spouses or cohabiting partners as between themselves.

NOTE: Because of the likelihood that this agreement may be more advantageous to one party than to the others it may be that the parties should be advised to have separate legal representation

THIS DEED OF AGREEMENT is made the .... day of ....19.........

BETWEEN:

1. *[name* ....*]* of *[address* ....*]* ("*[A]*") and

2. *[name* ....*]* of *[address* ....*]* ("*[B]*") and

3. *[name* ....*]* of *[address* ....*]* ("*[C]*")

WHEREAS:

(1) The parties [share] [intend to share] the Home (as defined below)

(2) The parties wish to enter into an agreement regulating their rights and obligations towards each other

(3) The parties intend that this Agreement shall be legally binding on them

(4) The parties declare that they have each had the benefit of independent legal advice prior to the execution of this agreement and are signing it voluntarily and in full understanding of their respective rights and liabilities hereunder.

OR

(4) The parties declare that they have been advised to seek independent legal advice but have declined to do so.

The Home

Existing Home

(5) [*name*] [is][are] presently resident at [address] ("the Home") which is a property purchased in the name[s] of *[name(s)*....................*]*

OR

Home to be purchased

(5) [*name*] are presently resident at the address[es] given above but intend to purchase a property ("the Home") in the name[s] of *[name(s) of owning party(ies)]* the address of which is *[address of the property to be purchased]*

IT IS HEREBY AGREED as follows:

The Home

1. The Home

(1) The Home [is] [will be] vested in the name[s] of *[name(s) of owning party(ies)]* and notwithstanding any contribution which *[name(s) of non-owning party(ies)]* may make directly or indirectly towards the purchase maintenance or improvement of the home [he][she][they] [has][have] and will acquire no beneficial interest whatsoever in the home

(2) From the date of this agreement *[name(s) of owning party(ies)]* as licensor[s] permit[s] *[name(s) of non-owning party(ies)]* to occupy the Home with [him][her][them] as licensee[s]. This licence is personal to *[name(s) of non-owning party(ies)]* and cannot be assigned. The licence shall determine on completion of any sale of the Home and *[name(s) of non-owning party(ies)]* shall vacate the Home and remove all [his][her][their] belongings on or before that date

NOTE: See note to agreement 3, clause 1

Outgoings

2. Outgoings

Common household expenditure including Council Tax or other local tax, water rates, gas, electricity, telephone, television licence and/or rental agreement, buildings household and contents insurance, food, decorating and repairs costing less than £1,000 shall be paid [equally] [as to *number* % by *A* and as to *number* % by *B* and as to *number* % by C] [by *name* alone]. [This provision shall also apply to payments of ground rent service charge(s) insurance premiums and any other sums due under the terms of any Lease by virtue of which the parties occupy the home]

NOTE: See note agreement 1 clause 7.

OR

2. *[Name of non-owning party]* will pay to *[name of owning party]* the sum of £.................per [week][calendar month] payable in advance on the first day of each [week][month] as a contribution towards the common household expenditure. This sum may be varied by agreement between the parties.

Contents

3. Ownership of Contents Options

Personal items and household items

(1) All items of personal use or adornment and all furniture household garden or garage articles or effects and electrical equipment shall belong to the party who last acquired them whether by inheritance gift or purchase

NOTE: This Clause has been drafted on the assumption that the parties would not wish to own items jointly as between all of them. Items owned jointly by spouses or partners will be covered by this Clause.

OTHER CLAUSE OPTIONS

If the parties wish to include in the agreement clauses dealing with motor vehicles, items acquired on credit, bank loans, overdrafts, credit cards or family loans precedents for these can be found in Agreement 1.

Accounts

4. Bank and Building Society accounts

Any joint Bank or Building Society account the parties may have or may establish in all their names for the purpose of paying the expenses hereinbefore referred to shall belong to the parties in equal shares [as to *[number]* % to *A* as to *[number]* % to *B* and as to *[number]* % to *C*]

NOTE: See note agreement 3 clause 11

Disputes

5. Dispute resolution

If there should be any dispute between the parties concerning this agreement (other than disputes about valuation when the provisions for resolution of such disputes contained elsewhere in this agreement shall apply) either during the subsistence of this agreement or upon termination hereof which the parties are not able to resolve themselves they agree to refer such dispute to mutually convenient mediators of the Family Mediators Association whilst reserving the right to refer the matter to the Court for adjudication if resolution of the dispute should not prove possible.

Termination/variation

6. Termination

This Agreement shall terminate on the happening of any of the following:

(a) The death of any party
(b) Notice in writing given by any party to the other[s] whereupon the transitional provisions below shall apply
(c) The parties agreeing mutually to cease to live together whereupon the transitional provisions below shall apply
(d) The abandonment of the home by any party and such abandonment being deemed by the other party[ies] to terminate the agreement whereupon the transitional provisions below shall apply

7. Transitional Provisions

In the event of this Agreement being terminated except by death the following transitional provisions shall apply:

(1) *[Name of non-owning party]*'s licence to occupy shall determine and [he][she] shall vacate the Home and remove all [his][her] belongings within *[insert number of days]* from the date of termination of the agreement or the death of *[name of owning party]*

(2) *[Name of non-owning party]* is entitled to a refund of that proportion of the [weekly][monthly] contribution already paid in respect of any period after [he][she] vacates the Home

8. Variation

Any variation of this Agreement shall only be effective if recorded in a supplemental written agreement executed by all parties

IN WITNESS WHEREOF the parties hereto have hereunto set their hands the day and year first before written

SIGNED AS A DEED
by the said

in the presence of

SIGNED AS A DEED
by the said

in the presence of

SIGNED AS A DEED
by the said

in the presence of

B.

DEEDS OF TRUST

DEED OF TRUST 3: PROPERTY IN ALL NAMES

THIS DEED OF TRUST is made the..day of ....19..........

BETWEEN:

1. *[name* ....*]* of *[address* ....*]* ("*[A]*") and

2. *[name* ....*]* of *[address* ....*]* ("*[B]*") and

3. *[name* ....*]* of *[address* ....*]* ("*[C]*") and

4. *A*, *B* and *C* ("the Trustees")

WHEREAS:

(1) By a [Transfer] [Conveyance] [dated.............] [of even date but executed before this Deed] and made between *[name of Vendor]* ("the Vendor") of the one part and the Trustees of the other part and in consideration of the payment of the sum of..............pounds (£............) the property described in the Schedule hereto ("the Home") was [Transferred] [Conveyed] to the Trustees in fee simple upon trust as therein stated

OR

(1) By a [Transfer] [Conveyance] [dated...................] [of even date but executed before this Deed] *[name(s)]* as existing owners [Transferred] [Conveyed] the property described in the Schedule hereto ("the Home") to the Trustees in fee simple upon trust as therein stated

OR

(1) By a Lease [dated...................] [of even date but executed before this Deed] and made between *[parties]* ("the Lease") the property described in the Schedule hereto ("the Home") was demised to [the Trustees] *[original lessee]* for the term of [...........] years from *[date]* at the yearly rent of £............subject to the terms and conditions of the Lease.

[By an Assignment [dated..........] [of even date but executed before this Deed] and made between *[assignor]* of the one part and the Trustees of the other part the Home is now vested in the Trustees for all the residue of the term of years granted by the Lease]

(2) By a Mortgage ("the Mortgage") [dated............] [of even date] [name(s)] charged the Home with the payment to *[name of Mortgagee]* as Mortgagees of the sum of.............pounds (£..........) with interest thereon and subject to the terms and conditions of the Mortgage

[and by a Deed [dated...............] [of even date] *[name(s)]* covenanted with the Mortgagees to be bound by the terms and conditions of the Mortgage]

Beneficial interest

Option A: Joint Tenants

(3) The parties have agreed that they are entitled to the beneficial interest in the Home as joint tenants in equity

OR

Option B: Equal Shares

(3) The parties have agreed that they are entitled to the beneficial interest in the Home as tenants in common as to *[number]* % to *A* and *B* which they shall hold as joint tenants in equity as between themselves and as to *[number]* % to *C* (This shall be the case regardless of the parties' respective contributions to the purchase price of the Home)

OR

Option C: % Shares

(3) The parties have agreed that they are entitled to the beneficial interest in the Home as to *[number]* % to *A* and as to *[number]* % to *B* and as to *[number]* % to *C*. (This shall be the case regardless of the parties' respective contributions to the purchase price of the Home)

OR

Option D: Shares in Proportion to Purchase Price/Mortgage

(3) The parties have agreed that they shall be entitled to the beneficial interest in the Home in the proportions ("the agreed proportions") in which they contribute to the purchase of the Home whether by way of payment of mortgage instalments as set out in Clause 1 and/or by way of future lump sum payment as set out in Clauses 2 and 4 of the Living Together Agreement [dated..............] [of even date] entered into by the parties ("the Agreement")

OR

Option E: Provision for previous contributions by one or more parties to be taken into account. Remainder in accordance with Agreement or in stated shares

(3) The parties have agreed that they shall be entitled to the beneficial interest in the Home in proportions ("the agreed proportions") calculated on the basis that:

(a) *A* is entitled to a sum equal to *[number]* % of the sale price before deductions or............pounds (£............) whichever is the greater as a result of having paid ....pounds (£.............)

AND/OR

B is entitled to a sum equal to *[number]* % of the sale price before deductions or..............pounds (£............) whichever is the greater as a result of having paid ....pounds (£............)

AND/OR

C is entitled to a sum equal to *[number]* % of the sale price before deductions or..............pounds (£............) whichever is the greater as a result of having paid ....pounds (£............)

AND/OR

[name] is entitled to a sum equal to *[number]* % of the sale price before deductions or.............pounds (£...........) whichever is the greater as a result of having obtained a discount in the purchase price due to [his] [her] [their] prior occupation of the Home as a tenant

AND/OR

[name] is entitled to a sum equal to *[number]* % of the sale price before deductions or.............pounds (£...........) whichever is the greater as a result of having obtained a reduction in the purchase price as a benefit from [his] [her] family

(b) The remainder shall be held in the proportions in which they contribute to the purchase of the Home whether by way of payment of mortgage instalments as set out in Clause 1 and/or by way of future lump sum payment as set out in Clauses 2 and 4 of the Living Together Agreement [dated...........] [of even date] entered into by the parties ("the Agreement")

OR

(b) The remainder shall be held as to *[number]* % for *A* and as to *[number]* % for *B* and as to *[number]* % for *C*

NOW THIS DEED WITNESSETH as follows:

1. The Trustees shall hold the Home on trust to sell the same with power to postpone the sale and shall hold the net rents and profits until sale and the net proceeds of sale (after deducting the balance of any monies due under the Mortgage for themselves

Option A: joint tenants

as joint tenants in equity

Option B: equal shares

as tenants in common as to *[number]* % to *A* and *B* which they shall hold as joint tenants in equity as between themselves and as to *[number]* % to *C*

Option C: percentage shares

as tenants in common as to *[number]* % for *A* and as to *[number]* % for *B* and as to *[number]* % for *C*

Options D and E: contributions/agreed proportions

as tenants in common in the agreed proportions

2. *A*, *B* and *C* HEREBY COVENANT with each other:

(a) To observe and perform all covenants restrictions conditions and stipulations at any time affecting the Home and the terms and conditions of the Mortgage [and of the Lease]

(b) To keep the Home and Contents insured against all usual comprehensive risks to the full reinstatement or replacement value of the same and to pay the insurance premiums in accordance with the terms of [the said Agreement] [the Living Together Agreement [dated...........] [of even date] entered into by *A*, *B* and *C* ("the Agreement")] and subject to the provisions of the Mortgage [and of the Lease] to apply any monies received on any policy of insurance effected on the home and contents in the replacement or reinstatement thereof

(c) That no party shall create or purport to create any charge mortgage lien or other interest (other than the Mortgage) in respect of the Home as a whole or their respective shares or to dispose by sale gift or otherwise of the whole or part of their respective shares without the consent in writing of the other parties

[except that this provision shall not restrict the right of any party to dispose of his or her share by Will]

NOTE: This alternative should be used if the parties hold the beneficial interest as tenants in common.

OR

[For the avoidance of doubt the parties declare that this provision shall not restrict the right of any of them to sever the equitable joint tenancy and subject thereto to dispose of his or her share by Will]

NOTE: This alternative should be used if the parties hold the beneficial interest as joint tenants.

(d) As between the parties the payment of monies due under the terms of the Mortgage [and of the Lease] and the funding of major repairs and improvements to the Home shall be as contained in the Agreement.

3. If either *A* or *B* or *C* or any of them (or their Personal Representatives) shall wish the Trust for sale to take effect he or she or they shall give notice to the other party or parties in accordance with the terms of the Agreement and the provisions as to the right of the other party or parties to purchase the whole of the Home and the manner of any sale shall be as contained in the Agreement

4. On completion of the sale of the Home (other than by way of purchase by one or more party or parties of the remaining share(s) the proceeds after deduction of all sums repayable under the Mortgage [outstanding under the Lease] and all expenses of sale shall belong to *A*, *B* and *C* in the proportions stated in Clause 1 above

IN WITNESS whereof the parties hereto have hereunto set their hands the day and year first before written

SCHEDULE

SIGNED AS A DEED
by the said

in the presence of

SIGNED AS A DEED
by the said

in the presence of

SIGNED AS A DEED
by the said

in the presence of

DEED OF TRUST 4: PROPERTY NOT IN ALL NAMES

THIS DEED OF TRUST is made the..day of ....19.......

BETWEEN:

[name(s)...*]* of *[address(es)*..*]* ("the Owner(s)") and

the Owner(s) and *[name(s)*...*]* of *[address(es)*......................................*]* ("the Beneficial Owners")

WHEREAS:

(1) By a [Transfer] [Conveyance] [dated............] [of even date but executed before this Deed] and made between *[name of Vendor...........]* ("the Vendor") of the one part and the Owner(s) of the other part and in consideration of the payment of the sum of .... pounds (£............) the property described in the Schedule hereto ("the Home") was [Transferred] [Conveyed] to the Owner(s) in fee simple [to the owners as trustees in fee simple upon trust as therein stated]

OR

(1) By a [Transfer] [Conveyance] [dated...........] [of even date but executed before this Deed] *[name(s)]* as existing owners [Transferred] [Conveyed] the property described in the Schedule hereto ("the Home") to the owners in fee simple upon trust as therein stated

OR

(1) By a Lease [dated............] [of even date but executed before this Deed] and made between *[parties]* ("the Lease") the property described in the Schedule hereto ("the Home") was demised to [the Owner(s)] *[original lessee]* for the term of [...........] years from *[date]* at the yearly rent of £..............subject to the terms and conditions of the Lease

[By an Assignment [dated...........] [of even date but executed before this Deed] and made between *[assignor]* of the one part and the Owner of the other part the Home is now vested in the Owner[s] for all the residue of the term of years granted by the Lease]

(2) By a Mortgage ("the Mortgage") [dated...............] [of even date] the Owner(s) charged the Home with the payment to *[name of mortgagee]* as Mortgagees of the sum of.............pounds (£............) with interest thereon and subject to the terms and conditions of the Mortgage

[and by a Deed [dated............] [of even date] *[name(s)]* covenanted with the Mortgagees to be bound by the terms and conditions of the Mortgage]

(3) The Owner[s][is][are] desirous of transferring the benefit of ownership in the Home to the Beneficial Owners so that the net proceeds of sale shall belong as from the date hereof to the Beneficial Owners as hereinafter stated

NOW THIS DEED WITNESSETH as follows:

1. The Owner[s] HEREBY DECLARE[S] that [he][she][they] hold[s] the Home on trust for the Beneficial Owners and hereby agree[s] that [he][she][they] will at the request and cost of the Beneficial Owners [transfer or convey] [assign] the same to such person or persons at such time or times and in such manner or otherwise deal with the same as the Beneficial Owners shall direct

2. The Beneficial Owners HEREBY COVENANT with each other:

(a) To observe and perform all covenants restrictions conditions and stipulations at any time affecting the Home and the terms and conditions of the Mortgage [and of the Lease]
(b) To keep the Home and Contents insured against all usual comprehensive risks to the full reinstatement or replacement value of the same and to pay the insurance premiums in accordance with the terms of the Living Together Agreement [dated..........] [of even date] entered into by the Beneficial Owners ("the Agreement") and subject to the provisions of the Mortgage [and of the Lease] to apply any monies received on any policy of insurance effected on the Home and Contents in the replacement or reinstatement thereof
(c) That no party shall create or purport to create any charge, mortgage lien or other interest (other than the Mortgage) in respect of the Home as a whole or their respective shares or to dispose by sale gift or otherwise of the whole or part of their respective shares without the consent in writing of the other party[ies]

[except that this provision shall not restrict the right of any party to dispose of his or her share by Will]

NOTE: See note deed of trust 1 clause 2 (c).

OR

[For the avoidance of doubt the parties declare this provision shall not restrict the right of any of them to sever the equitable joint tenancy and subject thereto to dispose of his or her share by Will]

NOTE: See note deed of trust 1 clause 2 (c).

(d) As between the parties the payment of monies due under the terms of the Mortgage [and of the Lease] and the funding of major repairs and improvements to the Home shall be as contained in the Agreement

3. If either *A* or *B* or *C* or any of them (or their Personal Representatives) shall wish the Home to be sold he or she or they shall give notice to the other party or parties in accordance with the terms of the Agreement and the provisions as to the right of the other party or parties to purchase the whole of the Home and the manner of any sale shall be as contained in the Agreement

4. On completion of the sale of the Home (other than by way of purchase by one or more parties of the remaining share[s], the proceeds of sale after deduction of all sums repayable under the Mortgage [outstanding under the Lease] and all expenses of sale shall belong to *A*, *B* and *C*

Option A: Joint Tenants

as joint tenants in equity

OR

Option B: Equal Shares

as tenants in common as to *[number]* % to *A* and *B* which they shall hold as joint tenants in equity as between themselves and as to *[number]* % to *C* (which shall be the case regardless of the parties' respective contributions to the purchase price of the Home)

OR

Option C: % Shares

as tenants in common as to *[number]* % for *A* as to *[number]* % for *B* and as to *[number]* % for *C* (which shall be the case regardless of the parties' respective contributions to the purchase price of the Home)

Option D: Contributions

as tenants in common in the proportions in which they contribute to the purchase of the Home whether by way of payment of mortgage instalments as set out in Clause 1 and/or by way of lump sum payment as set out in Clauses 2 and 4 of the Agreement

OR

Option E: Agreed Proportions

(a) as tenants in common in proportions calculated on the basis that:

A is entitled to a sum equal to *[number]* % of the sale price before deductions or ....pounds (£............) whichever is the greater as a result of having paid.............pounds (£............)

AND/OR

B is entitled to a sum equal to *[number]* % of the sale price before deductions or ....pounds (£............) whichever is the greater as a result of having paid.............pounds (£............)

AND/OR

C is entitled to a sum equal to *[number]* % of the sale price before deductions or.- ....pounds (£............) whichever is the greater as a result of having paid.............pounds (£............)

AND/OR

[name] is entitled to a sum equal to *[number]* % of the sale price before deductions or.............pounds (£............) whichever is the greater as a result of having obtained a discount in the purchase price due to [his] [her] [their] prior occupation of the Home as a tenant

AND/OR

[name] is entitled to a sum equal to *[number]* % of the sale price before deductions or.............pounds (£............) whichever is the greater as a result of having obtained a reduction in the purchase price as a benefit from [his] [her] family

(b) And the remainder in the proportions in which they contribute to the purchase of the Home whether by way of payment of mortgage instalments as set out in Clause 1 and/or by way of future lump sum payment as set out in Clauses 2 and 4 of the Agreement

OR

(b) And the remainder as to *[number]* % for *A* as to *[number]* % for *B* and as to *[number]* % for *C*

OR

Option F: Owner[s] to have benefit of value to date. Remainder in accordance with agreement

on the basis that *[name of non-owner(s)]* [is][are] not entitled to any beneficial interest in the Home as at the date of this Deed. The agreed value of the Home less the amount outstanding on the Mortgage as at the date hereof is..............pounds (£...............) and *[owner(s)]* shall be entitled to this sum out of the net proceeds of sale before division and in addition to any further share to which [he][she][they] may become entitled under the terms of the Agreement. From the date hereof *[non-owner(s)]* shall acquire a beneficial interest and hereafter the parties shall be entitled to the beneficial interest in the Home as tenants in common in the proportions in which they contribute to the purchase of the Home whether by way of payment of mortgage instalments as set out in Clause 1 and/or by way of future lump sum payment as set out in Clauses 2 and 4 of the Agreement

Option G: Owner[s] to have benefit of value at date of commencement of sharing arrangement. Remainder in accordance with agreement

on the basis that at the commencement of the sharing arrangement on or about *[date] [name of non-owner(s)]* had no beneficial interest in the Home. From the said date *[non-owner(s)]* acquired a beneficial interest. The agreed value of the Home less the amount outstanding on the mortgage as at the said date was..............pounds (£............) and *[owner(s)]* shall be entitled to this sum out of the net proceeds of sale before division and in addition to any further share to which [he][she][they] may become entitled under the terms of the Agreement. From the date hereof *[non-owner(s)]* shall acquire a beneficial interest and hereafter the parties shall be entitled to the beneficial interest in the Home in the proportions in which they contribute to the purchase of the Home whether by way of payment of mortgage instalments as set out in Clause 1 and/or by way of future lump sum payment as set out in Clauses 2 and 4 of the Agreement

OR

Option H: Owner[s] to have benefit of value to date. Remainder in stated shares

on the basis that *[name of non-owner(s)]* [is][are] not entitled to any beneficial interest in the Home as at the date of this Deed. The agreed value of the Home less the amount outstanding on the mortgage as at the date hereof is..............pounds (£............) and *[owner(s)]* shall be entitled to this sum out of the net proceeds of sale before division and in addition to [his] [her] [their] percentage share in any increase in value in the Home over and above the said sum. The parties declare that they are entitled to the beneficial interest in any increase in the value of the Home over and above the said sum as tenants in common as to *[number]* % to *A* as to *[number]* % to *B* and as to *[number]* % to *C*

OR

Option I: Owner[s] to have benefit of value at date of commencement of sharing arrangement. Remainder in stated shares

on the basis that at the commencement of the sharing arrangement on or about *[date][name of non-owner(s)]* had no beneficial interest in the Home. From the said date *[non-owner(s)]* acquired a beneficial interest. The agreed value of the Home less the amount outstanding on the mortgage as at the commencement of cohabitation on or about *[date]* was..............pounds (£............) and *[name of owner(s)]* shall be entitled to this sum out of the net proceeds of sale before division and in addition to [his][her][their] percentage share in any increase in value in the Home over and above the said sum. The parties declare that they are entitled to the beneficial interest in any increase in value of the Home over and above the said sum as tenants in common as to *[number]* % for *A* as to *[number]* % for *B* and as to *[number]* % for *C*

NOTE: See note agreement 1 recital 6 (F) to (I).

IN WITNESS whereof the parties hereto have hereunto set their hands the day and year first before written

SCHEDULE

SIGNED AS A DEED
by the said

in the presence of

SIGNED AS A DEED
by the said

in the presence of

SIGNED AS A DEED
by the said

in the presence of

SECTION 3
WILLS CLAUSES

WILLS CLAUSES

NOTE: These clauses have been included specifically to assist when advising cohabiting couples. Readers will no doubt already have Wills precedents which are suitable for the elderly client although some of the following clauses may be useful.

Executors

1. *Surviving Partner with two substituted if does not prove*

I APPOINT *[name...]* of *[address...]* to be the sole [Executor] [Executrix] and Trustee of this my Will but if [he] [she] shall predecease me or die without having proved it then I APPOINT *[name...]* of *[address.......................]* and *[name.....................]* of *[address.................]* to be the Executors and Trustees hereof AND I DECLARE that in the subsequent clauses of this my Will the expression "my Trustees" shall where the context admits mean and include the trustee or trustees hereof for the time being whether original additional or substituted

2. *Two Executors*

I APPOINT *[name...]* of *[address...]* and *[name...................]* of *[address.........................]* to be the Executors and Trustees of this my Will AND I DECLARE that in the subsequent clauses of this my Will the expression "my Trustees" shall where the context admits mean and include the trustee or trustees hereof for the time being whether original additional or substituted

NOTE: It is important to decide who, in practical terms, will have the responsibility for administering the deceased partner's estate. It is probably a good idea to appoint the surviving partner either alone (with substitution should he or she have predeceased) or with another Executor of the testator's choice.

Guardians

3. *Immediate Appointment*

I APPOINT [his] [her] [their] [father] *[name......................]* to be the guardian of my child[ren] *[name(s)...................]*

4. *After death of surviving former WIFE or HUSBAND*

If my former [wife] [husband] *[name...................]* shall die (whether or not in my lifetime) before my child[ren] *[name(s)...........]* shall have attained the age of majority then I APPOINT *[name...................]* to be guardian of my said child[ren] either alone or jointly with such person or persons as my said former [wife] [husband] may appoint

5. *Immediate appointment with substitution*

I APPOINT [his] [her] [their] [father] *[name...................]* to be the guardian of my child[ren] *[name(s)...................]* provided that if the said *[name...................]* shall die before my said child[ren] shall have attained the age of majority then I APPOINT *[name...................]* and *[name...................]* as substituted guardians

NOTE: There are two situations which may need consideration. The first is that either partner may have children by a previous (or still existing) marriage. He or she may wish to appoint a guardian or guardians of those children. Under the provisions of the Children Act 1989 the appointment takes effect only on the death of the surviving parent unless the Appointor already has a sole residence order. If this is the case the appointment takes effect on the death of the Appointor and the guardian then has joint parental responsibility with the survivor.

The second consideration is that even today, the father of a child born outside marriage has very few automatic rights. If there are children of the relationship therefore, the mother may wish to appoint the natural father as testamentary guardian. Since he cannot at present make an appointment, unless he has a Court Order or agreement giving him parental responsibility, they may wish to agree on a substituted appointment in the mother's will to take effect if both die during the children's minority.

It is probably a good idea for greater clarity to include the children's names rather than refer to them as a class.

NOTE: It is also possible to appoint a guardian by deed or, since the Children Act came into force, an appointment is effective if made in writing, dated and signed. (See Appointment of Guardian in Section 5).

Specific legacies

6. Outright gift of personal and household effects (including car)

I GIVE free of all Inheritance Tax and other fiscal impositions payable in respect of my estate and free of all costs of delivery all my furniture articles and effects of personal household domestic garage or garden use ornament or consumption [including any motor vehicle owned by me at the date of my death] not otherwise specifically disposed of by this my will or any Codicil hereto to *[name...................]* absolutely

NOTE: If the bulk of one partner's estate is not to go to the survivor, for example because it is to go to children, then the testator may wish to leave his/her household and personal effects to the surviving partner so as to avoid dispute as to who owns what and the need for replacement.

It is a good idea to make specific reference to the car since otherwise it may lead to dispute. If the car is likely to be subject to hire purchase then the words in square brackets in clause 6 should be deleted and the following clause included.

7. Car plus benefit of HP Agreement

I GIVE free of all Inheritance Tax and other fiscal impositions payable in respect of my estate any motor vehicle owned by me at the date of my death or held by me under any hire purchase agreement including the option to purchase conferred by such agreement to *[name...................]* AND I FURTHER DIRECT that my Trustees may if they think fit allow the said *[name...................]* to have custody of such motor vehicle pending discharge of any hire purchase agreement

AND

[AND I DIRECT that any sums remaining payable under such hire purchase agreement shall be paid from my Residuary Estate]

OR

[AND I DECLARE that the gift is conditional upon the said *[name...................]* discharging any sums remaining payable under such hire purchase agreement]

8. Benefit of Insurance Policy

I GIVE free of all Inheritance Tax and other fiscal impositions payable in respect of my estate the policy of insurance on my life with the *[Insurance Company's name...................]* dated [...................] and numbered [...................] and all bonuses and other sums payable in respect of the said policy to *[name...................]* absolutely

NOTE: One way of providing for dependants where there are several conflicting obligations is by life insurance. The benefit of the policy may be written in trust for the recipient or left by will using the above clause. The testator should check with his/her insurance company as to the available options.

The home

NOTE: If the residue of the estate is not to go to the surviving partner, then it may be helpful to look at the home, or the testator's share in it, as a separate item. The testator may be able to make an outright gift of the home (or his/her share if held as tenants in common) to the surviving partner. However, often the house is the main asset and some compromise may be needed.

9. *Life or Limited Interest*

(1) I GIVE [free of] [subject to] any mortgage or mortgages thereon and [free of] [subject to] all Inheritance Tax and other fiscal impositions payable thereon as a result of my death [my property] [all my share and interest in the property] *[address..................]* or such other dwellinghouse bungalow or flat which I may own either alone or jointly with *[name]* as beneficial tenants in common and which shall be my permanent residence at the date of my death ("the Property") to my Trustees UPON TRUST to sell the same with power to postpone the sale thereof so long as they shall in their absolute discretion think fit without being liable for loss

(2) I DIRECT that notwithstanding the trust for sale contained in this clause of my Will the Property shall not be sold during the lifetime of *[name]* PROVIDED that [she] [he] shall be residing permanently therein at the date of my death) without [his] [her] consent in writing until the first of the following to happen that is [his] [her] death [his] [her] remarriage [his] [her] cohabiting with a person of either sex not being a member of [his] [her] or my immediate family (but this condition shall not preclude normal short term visits by friends or relatives) and [his] [her] ceasing to reside in the Property ("the determining event") and that during such period the following provisions shall apply:

(a) No involuntary ceasing to reside in the Property by *[name]* shall be construed against [him] [her] as ceasing to reside therein for the purposes of this clause

(b) Until the determining event my Trustees shall allow *[name]* to occupy the same free of rent so long as [he] [she] shall desire but upon the terms that [he] [she] shall pay all rates taxes and other outgoings payable in respect thereof and shall keep the same in good repair and condition and insured in the names of my Trustees (or in the name of [himself] [herself] and my Trustees if joint) against such risks and in such amounts as my Trustees shall from time to time require

(c) It shall not be obligatory on my Trustees to see to the repair or insurance of the Property and they shall not be personally liable by reason of the neglect or omission of *[name]* to repair or insure the same or by reason of any loss resulting therefrom but nevertheless my Trustees may take such steps as they shall in their absolute discretion think fit for the protection and preservation of the Property and shall be entitled to be reimbursed out of the proceeds of sale of the Property when the same shall be sold for all expenses incurred by them in these respects but all moneys received (whether by *[name]* or by my Trustees) in respect of any insurance of the Property shall be forthwith applied in the replacement or reinstatement thereof

(d) If *[name]* being in occupation of the Property or of any dwellinghouse bungalow or flat purchased pursuant to this present sub-clause shall request my Trustees to sell the same or join in the sale of the Property if jointly owned my Trustees shall do so as soon as practicable thereafter and shall at the like request of *[name]* apply all or any part of the net proceeds of sale or share of the net proceeds of sale if jointly owned towards the purchase of another freehold or leasehold dwellinghouse bungalow or flat selected by *[name]* and approved by my Trustees and any residence so purchased shall be assured to my Trustees or to *[name]* and my Trustees as beneficial tenants in common if joint UPON TRUST to sell the same and the provisions of this clause shall apply to the residence so purchased as they apply to the Property AND I DECLARE for the avoidance of doubt that any part of the net proceeds of sale of the Property or share of the net proceeds if jointly owned not applied towards the purchase of another residence as aforesaid shall be held by my Trustees upon the trusts declared in the next succeeding sub-clause hereof and also that it is my intention that the purchase of any residence purchased in accordance with the provisions of this sub-clause shall be funded in the same proportions as the Property if the same is jointly owned

(3) SUBJECT as aforesaid my Trustees shall hold the net proceeds of sale and the net rents and profits until sale or share thereof if jointly owned of the Property

[UPON TRUST absolutely for such of them *[names..................]* as shall be living at my death and if more than one in equal shares]

OR

[UPON TRUST absolutely for such of them *[names..................]* as shall be living at the determining event and if more than one in equal shares]

OR

[UPON the trusts concerning my Residuary Estate hereinafter declared]

NOTE: The surviving partner may be given a life interest in the home so that he/she could continue living in the property but so that the capital value would pass eventually under the testator's will, eg to his/her children. This may be more appropriate where the partners are fairly elderly because otherwise it could tie up the capital for a considerable number of years and there can be problems over liability for maintenance of the property.

Clause (2): The aim of the third determining event is to bring the right to reside in the Home to an end should the surviving partner cohobit with someone else. There are obvious difficulties in satisfactorily defining "cohabitation" and also "immediate family".

Clause 2(d) gives the right to call for sale of the Home and purchase of another to be held on the same trusts.

Clause (3): If the remaindermen are identified as at the date of the testator's death it may make it easier to reach agreement if future problems arise, eg on the need to carry out structural repairs. Alternatively, the testator may prefer to name persons actually alive when the life interest finishes or is determined rather than risk the complications of predeceased remaindermen.

10. Provision for sale of House (or Share) to be postponed for a Specified Period

Notwithstanding the trust for sale concerning my Residuary Estate hereinafter contained I DIRECT that my Trustees shall not sell or call for the sale of [my property] [all my share and interest in the property] *[address..................]* or such other dwellinghouse bungalow or flat which I may own either alone or jointly with *[name]* as beneficial tenants in common and which shall be my permanent residence at the date of my death ("the Property") before the expiration of *[number]* months from the date of my death without the written consent of *[name]* (PROVIDED that [she] [he] shall survive me and shall be residing permanently therein at the date of my death) and that during such period the following provisions shall apply:

(a) Until the Property shall be sold my Trustee shall allow *[name]* to occupy the same free of rent upon the terms that [she] [he] shall pay all rates taxes and other outgoings payable in respect thereof and shall keep the same in good repair and condition and insured in the names of my Trustees against such risks and in such amounts as my Trustees shall from time to time require.

(b) It shall not be obligatory on my Trustees to see to the repair or insurance of the Property and they shall not be personally liable by reason of the neglect or omission of *[name]* to repair or insure the same or by reason of any loss resulting therefrom but nevertheless my Trustees may take such steps as they shall in their absolute discretion think fit for the protection and preservation of the Property and shall be entitled to be reimbursed out of the proceeds of sale of the Property when the same shall be sold for all expenses incurred by them in these respects but all moneys received (whether by *[name]* or by my Trustees) in respect of any insurance of the Property shall be forthwith applied in the replacement or reinstatement thereof

NOTE: A provision for the sale of the home to be postponed for a fixed period of time will allow the surviving partner time to arrange other accommodation without having to rely on the goodwill of the residuary beneficiaries.

It is possible that the Inland Revenue may (particularly if the period of postponement exceeds six months) treat the end of the period as causing a transfer of value by the surviving partner and this possibility should be borne in mind.

11. Option to Purchase House (or Share)

MY Trustees shall by notice in writing offer *[name..................]* [my property *address*................][my share and interest in the property *address*................] which property I own jointly with *[name]* as tenants in common] or such other dwellinghouse bungalow or flat which I may own either alone or jointly with *[name]* as beneficial tenants in common at the date of my death ("the Property") to *[name]* for the purchase of the same by [him] [her] at a price to be determined by a Valuer appointed jointly by my Trustees and *[name]* or in default of agreement by a Valuer appointed by the President for the time being of the Royal Institution of Chartered Surveyors such offer to be made within four months of the date of my death and to be accepted by *[name]* within four months from the receipt of the notice by [him] [her] but notwithstanding anything herein contained the right of *[name]* to exercise the option by accepting such offer shall absolutely cease on the expiration of eight months from the date of my death

I FURTHER DECLARE that:

(a) the option is personal to *[name]* and shall be exercised by [him] [her] during [his] [her] lifetime and not by any person (including [his] [her] personal representatives) after [his] [her] death

(b) any Inheritance Tax or other fiscal impositions payable in respect of the Property on or by reason of my death shall be paid out of my Residuary Estate

(c) upon *[name]* exercising the option [she] [he] shall be entitled to a conveyance of the fee simple of the Property or of my beneficial share if jointly owned [she] [he] paying such costs as are paid by a purchaser for value. The Property shall be vested in [him] [her] free from incumbrances capable of being discharged by money payment and such incumbrances (if any) together with the costs of discharging the same (or my joint share of such incumbrances and costs) shall be discharged out of my residuary Estate

(d) upon the sale or other transaction by my Trustees in respect of or relating to the Property after the expiration of eight months from the date of my death a statement in writing by my Trustees that the option hereby given has not been exercised shall in favour of a purchaser or other person dealing with my Trustees for money or money's worth be conclusive evidence of the fact so stated

Residue

12. Residue for partner – substitution trust for sale to several named persons in equal shares

I GIVE

[all my real and personal estate whatsoever and wheresoever situate]

OR

[all the rest residue and remainder of my estate both real and personal whatsoever and wheresoever situate]

(subject to and after the payment thereout of my funeral and testamentary expenses and debts and all Inheritance Tax and other fiscal impositions payable in respect of my estate):
(a) to *[name]* absolutely if [her] [she] shall survive me for a period of twenty-eight days

(b) if the said *[name]* shall predecease me or shall not survive me for the said period of twenty-eight days then to my Trustees:

(i) UPON TRUST as to such estate (which together with the property for the time being representing the same is hereinafter referred to as "my Residuary Estate") to sell the same or any part thereof or to retain the same or any part thereof in its actual state of investment or condition at the date of my death without being liable for loss and

(ii) TO HOLD my Residuary Estate as to both capital and income UPON TRUST absolutely for such of the following persons namely *[names..................]* as shall be living at my death and if more than one in equal shares

13. Residue – trust for sale to several named persons in shares of unequal size or subject to different provisions

I GIVE
[all my real and personal estate whatsoever and wheresoever situate]

OR

[all the rest residue and remainder of my estate both real and personal whatsoever and wheresoever situate]

(subject to and after the payment thereout of my funeral and testamentary expenses and debts and all Inheritance Tax and other fiscal impositions payable in respect of my estate) to my Trustees:
(1) UPON TRUST as to such estate (which together with the property for the time being representing the same is hereinafter referred to as "my Residuary Estate") to sell the same or any part thereof or to retain the same or any part thereof in its actual state of investment or condition at the date of my death without being liable for loss and

(2) TO HOLD my Residuary Estate as to both capital and income UPON TRUST to divide the same into *[number..................]* equal shares and to stand possessed thereof upon trust absolutely:

(a) as to *[number................................]* such shares for *[name ....]*

(b) as to *[number................................]* such shares for *[name ....]*

(c) as to *[number................................]* such shares for *[name..]*

IF any share or shares of my Residuary Estate shall be undisposed of by reason of the lapse of any gift contained in the foregoing clause of this my Will such share or shares shall sink into my Residuary Estate and be held for the other person or persons entitled to the remaining shares in the proportions which such remaining shares bear to one another

NOTE: The last paragraph of this clause is to ensure that, having split the residue into separate shares, the failure of anyone to take an interest in a particular share will not result in a partial intestacy.

If there are only two shares the wording can be adapted appropriately.

This clause allows the separate shares to be subject to different provisions, eg differing substitution. (Example: The testator may wish to leave half to his partner and half to his children. He may also wish to provide that, should his partner predecease, her share or some of it goes to her family whereas his children's share would include normal per stirpes stipulation.)

It is probably a good idea always to incorporate a survivorship clause in respect of any gift to a partner.

14. Residue – trust for sale to several named persons in equal shares

I GIVE

[all my real and personal estate whatsoever and whersoever situate]

OR

[all the rest residue and remainder of my estate both real and personal whatsoever and wheresoever situate]

(subject to and after the payment thereout of my funeral and testamentary expenses and debts and all Inheritance Tax and other fiscal impositions payable in respect of my estate) to my Trustees:

(1) UPON TRUST as to such estate (which together with the property for the time being representing the same is hereinafter referred to as "my Residuary Estate") to sell the same or any part thereof or to retain the same or any part thereof in its actual state of investment or condition at the date of my death without being liable for loss and

(2) TO HOLD my Residuary Estate as to both capital and income UPON TRUST absolutely for such of the following persons namely *[names...................]* as shall be living at my death and if more than one in equal shares

SECTION 4

MISCELLANEOUS

Parental Responsibility Agreement

Date Recorded

Section 4(1)(b) The Children Act 1989

- ▶ **Please use black ink.**
- ▶ **The making of this agreement will seriously affect the legal position of both parents. You should both seek legal advice before completing this form.**
- ▶ **If there is more than one child, you should fill in a separate form for each child.**

THE — CHILDREN — ACT

This is a parental responsibility agreement between

the child's mother	*Name*
and	*Address*
the child's father	*Name*
	Address

We agree that the father of the child named below should have parental responsibility for [him] [her] in addition to the mother.

Name	Boy/Girl	Date of birth	Date of 18th birthday

Ending of the agreement

Once a parental responsibility agreement has been made it can only end:

- by an order of the court made on application of any person who has parental responsibility for the child.
- by an order of the court made on the application of the child with leave of the court.
- when the child reaches the age of 18.

Signed (**mother**)		Date	
Signature **of witness**)		Date	
Signed (**father**)		Date	
Signature **of witness**)		Date	

This agreement will not take effect until this form has been filed with the Principal Registry of the Family Division. Once this form has been completed and signed please take or send it and two copies to:

The Principal Registry of the Family Division
Somerset House
Strand
London WC2R 1LP

THE — CHILDREN — ACT

APPOINTMENT OF GUARDIAN

other than by Will

1. *Appointment of unmarried father*

I [name] of [address] appoint [his] [her] [their] father [name] [also] of [address] to be the guardian of my child[ren] [names] such appointment to take effect on my death

DATED ....

SIGNED ....

2. *Appointment of non-parent*

[I][WE] [name(s)] of [address] appoint [name(s)] of [address] to be the guardian[s] of [my][our][child[ren] [name(s)] such appointment to take effect on the death of the last surviving person with parental responsibility for such child[ren]

DATED ....

SIGNED ....

NOTE: It is usual for the appointment of a guardian to be made within the formality of a Will. However, Children Act 1989, s. 5 enables the appointment to be made in writing and signed and this may be appropriate in certain circumstances. For example, it allows a mother who is aged under 18 years, who cannot normally make a Will, to appoint a guardian. It also may encourage people who are reluctant to make Wills to make such an appointment.

MEMORANDUM OF GIFT

WE HEREBY DECLARE that on the.. day of............... 19 *[Name of donor(s)]* of *[address(es)]* gave to *[name(s) of donee(s)]* of *[address(es)]* the sum of.. pounds (£*number*) for the benefit of the donee(s) and stated the same to be a gift which the donee(s) accepted as such

....

SIGNED *(by all the parties)*

....

DATED

....

Form prescribed in the Schedule to The Enduring Powers of Attorney (Prescribed Form) Regulations 1990

Enduring Power of Attorney

Part A: About using this form

1. **You may choose one attorney or more than one.** If you choose one attorney then you must delete everything between the square brackets on the first page of the form. If you choose more than one, you must decide whether they are to be able to act:

   - Jointly (that is, they must all act together and cannot act separately) or
   - Jointly and severally (that is, they can all act together but they can also act separately if they wish).

   On the first page of the form, show what you have decided by crossing out one of the alternatives.

2. **If you give your attorney(s) general power** in relation to all your property and affairs, it means that they will be able to deal with your money or property and may be able to sell your house.

3. **If you don't want your attorney(s) to have such wide powers,** you can include any restrictions you like. For example, you can include a restriction that your attorney(s) must not act on your behalf until they have reason to believe that you are becoming mentally incapable; or a restriction as to what your attorney(s) may do. Any restrictions you choose must be written or typed where indicated on the second page of the form.

4. **If you are a trustee** (and please remember that co-ownership of a home involves trusteeship), you should seek legal advice if you want your attorney(s) to act as a trustee on your behalf.

5. **Unless you put in a restriction preventing it** your attorney(s) will be able to use any of your money or property to make any provision which you yourself might be expected to make for their own needs or the needs of other people. Your attorney(s) will also be able to use your money to make gifts, but only for reasonable amounts in relation to the value of your money and property.

6. **Your attorney(s) can recover the out-of-pocket expenses** of acting as your attorney(s). If your attorney(s), are professional people, for example solicitors or accountants, they may be able to charge for their professional services as well. You may wish to provide expressly for remuneration of your attorney(s) (although if they are trustees they may not be allowed to accept it).

7. **If your attorney(s) have reason in the future to believe** that you have become or are becoming mentally incapable of managing your affairs, your attorney(s) will have to apply to the Court of Protection for registration of this power.

8. **Before applying to the court of Protection for registration** of this power, your attorney(s) must give written notice that that is what they are going to do, to you and your nearest relatives as defined in the Enduring Powers of Attorney Act 1985. You or your relatives will be able to object if you or they disagree with registration.

9. **This is a simplified explanation** of what the Enduring Powers of Attorney Act 1985 and the Rules and Regulations say. If you need more guidance, you or your advisers will need to look at the Act itself and the Rules and Regulations. The Rules are the Court of Protection (Enduring Powers of Attorney) Rules 1986 (Statutory Instrument 1986 No 127). The Regulations are the Enduring Powers of Attorney (Prescribed Form) Regulations 1990 (Statutory Instrument 1990 No 1376).

10. **Note to Attorney(s)**
    After the power has been registered the attorney(s) should notify the Court of Protection if the donor dies or recovers.

11. **Note to Donor**
    Some of these explanatory notes may not apply to the form you are using if it has been adapted to suit your particular requirements.

YOU CAN CANCEL THIS POWER AT ANY TIME BEFORE IT HAS TO BE REGISTERED.

Part B: To be completed by the 'donor' (the person appointing the attorney(s))

Don't sign this form unless you understand what it means.

Please read the notes in the margin which follow and which are part of the form itself.	
Donor's name and address	I ______________________ of ______________________
Donor's date of birth	born on ______________________
See note 1 on the front of this form. If you are appointing only one attorney, you should cross out everything between the square brackets. If appointing more than 2 attorneys please give the additional name(s) on an attached sheet.	appoint ______________________ of ______________________ • [and ______________________ of ______________________
Cross out the one which does not apply (see note 1 on the front of this form).	1. • jointly • jointly and severally] to be my attorney(s) for the purposes of the Enduring Powers of Attorney Act 1985
Cross out the one which does not apply (see note 2 on the front of this form). Add any additional powers.	• with general authority to act on my behalf • with authority to do the following on my behalf
If you don't want the attorney(s) to have general power, you must give details here of what authority you are giving the attorney(s).	
Cross out the one which does not apply.	in relation to • all my property and affairs • the following property and affairs:

Part B: continued

Please read the notes in the margin which follow and which are part of the form itself.

If there are restrictions or conditions, insert them here; if not, cross out these words if you wish. (See note 3 on the front of this form)

If this form is being signed at your direction:
- the person signing must not be an attorney or any witness (to Parts B or C).
- you must add a statement that this form has been signed at your direction.
- a second witness is necessary (please see below).

Your signature (or mark).

Date.

Someone must witness your signature.

Signature of witness.

Your attorney(s) cannot be your witness. It is **not** advisable for your husband or wife to be your witness.

A second witness is only necessary if this form is not being signed by you personally but at your direction (for example, if a physical disability prevents you from signing).

Signature of second witness.

2 • subject to the following restrictions and conditions:

I intend that this power shall continue even if I become mentally incapable.

I have read or have had read to me the notes in Part A which are part of, and explain, this form.

Signed by me as a deed and delivered ________________

on ________________

In the presence of ________________

Full name and witness ________________

Address of witness ________________

In the presence of ________________

Full name of witness ________________

Address of witness ________________

Part C: To be completed by the attorney(s)

Note: 1. This form may be adapted to provide for execution by a corporation

2. If there is more than one attorney additional sheets in the form as shown below must be added to this **Part C**.

Please read the notes in the margin which follow and which are part of the form itself.

Don't sign this form before the donor has signed Part B or if, in your opinion, the donor was already mentally incapable at the time of signing Part B.

I understand that I have a duty to apply to the Court for the registration of this form under the Enduring Powers of Attorney Act 1985 when the donor is becoming or has become mentally incapable.

I also understand my limited power to use the donor's property to benefit persons other than the donor.

I am not a minor

If this form is being signed at your direction:
- the person signing must not be an attorney or any witness (to Parts B or C).
- you must add a statement that this form has been signed at your direction.
- a second witness is necessary (please see below).

*Signature (or mark) of attorney

†Date

Signature of witness

The attorney must sign the form and his signature must be witnessed. The donor may not be the witness and one attorney may not witness the signature of the other

Signed by me as a deed
and delivered* ______________________

on† ______________________

in the presence of ______________________

Full name of witness ______________________

Address of witness ______________________

____

____

____

A second witness is only necessary if this form is not being signed by you personally but at your direction (for example, if a physical disability prevents you from signing).

Signature of second witness

in the presence of ______________________

Full name of witness ______________________

Address of witness ______________________

____

____

____

PERSONAL CARE DECLARATION AND APPOINTMENT OF PERSONAL CARE DECISION-MAKER

I, *[name]*
of *[address]*
born on *[date of birth]*
MAKE THIS DECLARATION of my wishes as to my personal care to take effect in the event that a qualified medical practitioner certifies that I have through physical or mental incapacity become unable to make decisions myself as to my personal care or that as a result of such incapacity I have become unable to communicate those decisions to others.

I APPOINT *[name]* of *[address]* to be my personal care decision-maker with power to deal with and make all decisions concerning the following matters:-

(a) Where I am to live (should it become impossible or undesirable, in the opinion of my personal decision-maker after taking medical advice, for me to remain in my home until my death which otherwise would be my overriding wish)

(b) Whether I am to have such medical treatment as may be recommended by a qualified medical practitioner (subject to any wishes I may have expressed in a Living Will)

(c) To read my personal deeds, documents, papers and letters whether in my possession or in the possession of third parties [with the exception of my Will and any Codicils thereto]

(d) To exercise my rights to obtain such information [relating to me] as may be held by third parties

(e) [Other – such as exercise of religious observance, dietary wishes e.g. vegetarianism, wishes as to pets]

I UNDERSTAND that this declaration is not binding but is simply an expression of my wishes.

SIGNED this....................day of 19
By *[name]*
in the presence of:

I *[name]* have discussed my appointment with the Appointor and consent to such appointment

SIGNED by *[name]*
in the presence of:

APPOINTMENT OF PERSONAL CARE DECISION-MAKER
(General)

I, *[name]*
of *[address]*
born on *[date of birth]*
MAKE THIS DECLARATION of my wishes as to my personal care to take effect in the event that a qualified medical practitioner certifies that I have through physical or mental incapacity become unable to make decisions myself as to my personal care or that as a result of such incapacity I have become unable to communicate those decisions to others.

I APPOINT *[name]* of *[address]* to be my personal care decision-maker with general power to deal with and make all decisions concerning my personal care and welfare *save for the following:*

I UNDERSTAND that this declaration is not binding but is simply an expression of my wishes.

SIGNED this....................day of 19
By *[name]*
in the presence of:

SECTION 5
CHECK LISTS

CHECKLIST

File no
Fee earner ....

Clients' names ....

Clients advised on question of independent legal advice ☐

Currently owned property

Deeds with..
Authority sent (date) ....
Follow up (date) ....
Deeds received (date) ....

House being purchased

Memo to conveyancing dept (date) ....
Follow up (date) ....
Details of title received (date) ....

COMPLETION DATE

Wills

Wills with...
Authority sent (date) ....
Follow up (date) ....
Wills received (date) ....

Documents drafted

Agreement ☐
Deed of Trust ☐
Wills ☐
Memo of severance ☐

Drafts to clients (date) ....

Any amendments Yes No

Documents engrossed ....

Documents signed

Agreement (date) ....
Memo of severance ....
Wills ....
Deed of trust..

NOTE: If completion of a property being purchased is delayed then the deed of trust may be signed at a later date.

Wills and agreement to strongroom ☐
Letter to clients confirming ☐

Deeds – Registered title

Land charge cert ☐
Memo of severance ☐
Land registry fee ☐

} To land registry

Deeds – Unregistered title

Land/charge cert returned ....

Deeds, deed of trust and copy agreement } to Mortgagee ☐ OR Strongroom ☐

PERSONAL DETAILS – COHABITEES

Date ....
File No ....
Fee earner ....

Clients

Full name:	Full name:
Address:	Address:
Phone no:	Phone no:
Date of birth:	Date of birth:
Single/Married Divorced/Widowed	Single/Married Divorced/Widowed

Is either of the above properties being sold? Yes/No

Children

From a previous marriage/relationship:		From a previous marriage/relationship:	
Full name	Date of birth	Full name	Date of birth
Do they live with you?	Yes/no	Do they live with you?	Yes/no

Of this relationship:

Full name	Date of birth

Previous/Existing marriage

If you have previously been married is divorce final?	Yes/No	If you have previously been married is divorce final?	Yes/No
Has any order been made dealing with children or financial matters?	Yes/No	Has any order been made dealing with children or financial matters?	Yes/No
If Yes, details:		If Yes, details:	

LIVING TOGETHER QUESTIONNAIRE
PERSONAL DETAILS – SHARING WITH THE ELDERLY

Date ....
File No ....
Fee earner ....

Clients

Full name:
Address: Phone no:
Date of birth:
Single/Married Divorced/Widowed

Full name:
Address: Phone no:
Date of birth:
Single/Married Divorced/Widowed

Full name:
Address: Phone no:
Date of birth:
Single/Married Divorced/Widowed

Are any of the above properties being sold? Yes/No

QUESTIONNAIRE

The home

Address ....

If rented – in whose name(s)...

If being purchased – in whose name(s) ....
– how is it being funded?...

If joint: ☐ Joint tenants
☐ Tenants in common
(Intended shares? ....)

If already owned – in whose name(s) ....
– contributions ....

If joint: ☐ Joint tenants
☐ Tenants in common
(What shares?...)

Is this to be severed? Yes/No

If not in all names – is legal title to be transferred? Yes/No

Where are the deeds?...

If mortgage, account no:...

How do you want to own the beneficial shares?

- Joint tenants ☐
- Tenants in common – equal shares ☐
- Tenants in common – % shares ☐
- Shares in proportion ☐
- Tenancy discount – allowance ☐
- Family discount – allowance ☐
- Sole name – other party's acquisition ☐

Do you want the following to affect your shares?

- Lump sum payment off mortgage ☐
- Improvements ☐
- Non-monetary contributions ☐
- Major repairs ☐

Is there a mortgage-linked endowment policy? Yes/No

Whose name(s) ....

Name of company ....

Policy no: ....

Is there a mortage protection policy? Yes/No

Payments

	Equally	A %	B %	C %	By one party
Mortgage and endowent policy premium					
Major repairs					
Rent					
Outgoings					

(Point out definitions of outgoings, arrangements for payment and effect of failure to pay)

Fixed contribution to common household expenditure | £ | A/B/C | PW/PCM |

Contents (for cohabitees)

Do you want these to include cars? | Yes/No |

Ownership	Joint	By the person who acquired them	All items over £..............to acquirer, rest joint

Items bought on credit over £.............................to be joint

Schedule – any specific items | Yes/No | List

Credit and loans (for cohabitees)

	Equally	Mr %	Ms %	By one party
Credit repayments (sole name)				
Credit repayments (joint/authorised User)				
Family loans (repayments)				

	Joint	One Party
Family loans (liability)		

Bank and building society accounts/investments and other assets (for cohabitees)

	Owned Equally	Owned Mr %	Owned Ms %
Joint			

(Point out sole account to remain sole)

Children (for cohabitees)		
Parental responsibility agreement		Yes/No
Provisions for payment if reduction in income	?Months	To be agreed
Maintenance payable	Joint liability	Sole liability

Termination

(Point out events for termination provisions in termination clause)

Mortgage payments	As existing	Party in occupation
Family loans repayment	As existing	Party whose family provided loan
Refund of proportion of fixed contribution to common household expenditure		Yes/No

Variation

(Point out variation only by supplemental agreement)

Other Documents?

Memorandum of Gift	Yes/No
Enduring Power of Attorney	Yes/No
Personal care declaration and appointment	Yes/No

LIVING TOGETHER QUESTIONNAIRE (WILLS)

Date ....

File no ....

Fee earner ....

Client's name: Mr/Ms/Mrs ....

Appointment of executors	**Full names/addresses/ relationship (if any)**	
Partner with 2 substituted if does not prove	☐	
Two executors	☐	
Other	☐	
Appointment of guardians		
Guardian(s)	☐	
Guardian(s) to take effect on death of surviving parent	☐	
Guardian with substitution	☐	
Other	☐	
Specific legacies		Tick if under 18
Household and personal effects	☐	
Car	☐	
Jewellery	☐	
Other	☐	

Pecuniary legacies

Amount	Full names/address/ relationship, if any	Tick if under 18

Provisions for house (or share)

Partner to have indefinite right to occupy ☐

Sale delayed for ☐ months ☐

NOTE: See note to Wills Clauses 10 as to possible Capital Tax implications

Option to purchase ☐

On sale, proceeds to ☐ fall into residue

☐ go to ....

NOTE: Suggest make household and personal effects specific gift rather than include in trust.

Residue

Cremation/burial instructions Yes/No Details ....

Existing will? Yes/No Where? ....